Under the Eye of the Shepherd

Under the Eye of the Shepherd

by
Werner Klein

with a foreword by Joy Robinson

CFI

Springville, Utah

© 2005 Werner Klein

ISBN: 1-55517-905-3
v.1

Published by CFI,
an imprint of Cedar Fort, Inc.
925 N. Main, Springville, Utah, 84663
www.cedarfort.com

Distributed by:

Cover design by Nicole Williams
Cover design © 2005 by Lyle Mortimer

Printed in the United States of America
10 9 8 7 6 5 4 3 2 1

Printed on acid-free paper.

To Mutti and Elschen

Contents

Foreword

I met Werner Klein and was introduced to his story in a rather miraculous way. I was four days away from deadline on *Touched by the Spirit* when a friend called and told me she thought I should meet Mr. Klein. He had written a book that he hoped I would read.

I was interested, but just then I had no time for reading. I asked her to have Mr. Klein call me, thinking we could make an appointment, which did happen. We made the appointment for two weeks; I was at the point of saying good-bye when a voice I have become familiar with said, "Get the book today." I quickly spoke before Werner hung up and asked if he could bring his book to me that day—all the while thinking how crazy I was because my book was not quite finished and I needed the days I had left.

I met Werner and his lovely wife, Linda. He gave me the book and I stayed up until 1:30 A.M. reading it. The Spirit had been active during the entire process of putting my book together, and other miraculous things had happened as I searched for spiritual stories. So I should not have been surprised when I found two beautiful stories in his manuscript that fit perfectly in my book. I asked for Mr. Klein's permission to use them, and he graciously consented.

Editing *Under the Eye of the Shepherd* and getting it ready for publication has been a wondrous learning experience. Four of my uncles were actively involved in World War II. One of them was a B-29 navigator stationed in London. He flew in more than fifty of the bombing missions that destroyed much of Europe and nearly all of Germany.

Werner and I were both children then, but our experiences during that devastating period are quite different. In America we had ration cards for food; he and his people were starving. We had ration cards for fuel; all private vehicles in Germany were commandeered by the military.

His story as a boy growing up in a country that was slowly being decimated by war touched me to the depths of my soul.

I have wept over this young boy and marveled at his inner strength and determination. Werner believes, as I do, that his strength came through the Lord and his mother's prayers. When he was captured and taken away, his mother continually prayed that the Lord's eye would be upon him, that he would be preserved, and that somehow he would find a way to escape and come home.

—*Joy Robinson*

Preface

Today, sixty years later, as I reflect upon the experiences I have related in this book, I realize how blessed I am that the Lord did watch over me and my family during times of often unbelievable agony, trials, and tribulations. Because of His watchful eye, care and concern, I am still alive and able to tell my story to others.

While living in California, I was asked to give several fireside talks about these experiences to members of The Church of Jesus Christ of Latter-day Saints, old and young alike.

I have often talked to both elementary and high school students in Utah, and I have been invited by teachers of history classes to share my story. Whenever I have the opportunity to talk to people, I always end my remarks with my testimony of how the Lord did answer my mother's prayers and my own by protecting us and saving our lives.

While the Prophet Joseph Smith was a prisoner at the jail in Liberty, Missouri, he pleaded with the Lord for help—for himself and the suffering Saints. The Lord gave him this answer: "Know thou, my son, that all these things shall give thee experience, and shall be for thy good" (D&C 122:7).

I feel also that the experiences I had strengthened my testimony and my faith; these trials helped me to grow in the gospel of Jesus Christ, and were for my own good. For this I will be ever grateful to my Lord and Savior—the Shepherd—who kept a lonely boy ever within his sight and under His protecting care.

CHAPTER ONE_____

The Beginning Years

In 1929, a calamity forever known as the Great Depression struck every nation in Europe. The depression caused untold suffering among the people, particularly those who were poor and must work for a living. Many German families were poor during this period of time. We were one of those families, and that is the year of my birth.

My mother, Emma, was thirty-three years old when I was born; my father, Emil, was thirty-seven. They were both born in Memel, East Prussia. Memel was the chief port of the Baltic Sea and was on the border of Russia. It was once an independent country called Lithuania. In 1386 it was occupied by Poland, then in 1772 by Russia. In 1919 Memel once more became an independent republic. But the independence was short lived because in 1940 it was taken over by the Soviet Union.

We were members of The Church of Jesus Christ of Latter-day Saints. My parents joined the Church when they lived in East Prussia. Missionaries from Salt Lake City found them while proselyting. They were baptized in the Baltic Sea; my mother often told us, "On a beautiful day, the setting sun touched the water with golden rays that reached out to where I stood, waiting for baptism."

Eventually there were four children in our family. Horst was born in 1924, Siegfried in 1926, myself in 1929, and Elsa in 1932. I was the third child, born between Siegfried and Elsa, a fact which undoubtedly saved my life.

By the time Elsa and I were born, the family was living in a town in Germany called Landsberg. We children were baptized at the age of eight. Both my baptism and my sister Elsa's took place in the Warthe River just outside the town of Landsberg.

At the time, Germany was a socialistic republic. My father was unable to find work for a number of years. There was a small amount of money given monthly to those who were unemployed. Medical care and hospitalization were free. Housing was very cheap. We were fortunate to own our home, though it was small; it had a kitchen, living room, and one bedroom, where we children slept. Our parents slept in the living room. There was no toilet. Our house was located just behind a large apartment building with a courtyard separating us. On the first floor of the apartment building there was a toilet room that our family used. We bathed in a large tub in the kitchen using heated water from a kettle.

The branch of the Church in Landsberg was small—about twenty members. We met in the back room of a downtown office building that was not being used. My father held the priesthood as an Elder. The members in our branch were like family, always looking out for each other. Our branch president was a shoemaker. The Relief Society president was an older lady who had a husband but no family. Her husband was a fisherman. She often called the children in our family to come and eat some fish her husband had caught. This was a wonderful thing for us because during most of our youth we children went to bed hungry. When we ate, there was barely enough for each person to have a small portion of whatever our mother prepared. We could never get filled, so we were always thinking and dreaming of food. When going to sleep, I would sometimes think of a favorite meal I would like to have and then dream that I was eating it.

We had what was called black bread, which was made with whole wheat and rye flour.

One part of our diet was fresh or salted herring that my mother got at the market. Herring came in big barrels and was transported to us by wagon from the seacoast. Herring and potatoes made up most of the diet for poor Germans at that time. Sometimes we could buy a little piece of meat and have a stew. We also had sauerkraut, which came to the market in big barrels. I did not like sauerkraut, but it was good for us, so our mother insisted that I eat it.

About the year 1935, the government gave land to families who wanted to have gardens and keep a few small animals. Each family received a half acre, which was located on a hill above our town. My father loved gardening and was very good at growing things. He planted tomatoes, green beans, corn, potatoes, and cabbage. We had fruit trees, and we also began raising chickens, rabbits, and a goat. Milk from the goat helped our family to have better health, and we were also able to sell some of the milk. Our life began to be a little better then.

The older boys had jobs that brought in some income for the family. I helped my father with the garden and with the animals. As Elsa grew older, she helped too.

It was necessary to carry buckets of water from our home up the hill to where the garden and animals were because the well was near the house. Work was hard for us and left no time for playing with other children. This is one of the reasons that Elsa and I became best friends, even though there was a difference in our age. We also shared the same interest in nature and love for animals. We grew up with farm animals—dogs and cats also—and always liked caring for them.

We depended on each other because we had nobody else.

In the evenings after day's end, Elsa and I would often sit together in a dark corner and sing our beloved folk songs. Elsa had a beautiful voice, and we harmonized together, our voices blending nicely. These times were some of our sweetest memories of childhood.

When winter came, we had more time for ourselves because there was no farm work to do other than carrying water to the animals. We enjoyed ice-skating and sleigh rides. We were too poor to buy a sled. Our father built one for us so we could go down the little hills and sometimes over bumps, which gave us fun and enjoyment. We went ice-skating on a nearby pond in a park. The city workers filled the pond with water for this purpose. We skated on the ice until dark, coming home with soaking wet socks because we did not have good winter boots. At other times, we would jump on horse-drawn sleds for an exciting ride down our narrow streets.

There are three incidents from my childhood that stand out clearly. One happened when I was about seven. The river Warthe ran not far from where we lived. One warm day, I took Elsa down to wade in the shallow water that was close to the bank. I could not swim. I happily splashed and played where I felt safe. Elsa was sitting at the edge of the water making mud houses.

Suddenly, I dropped into a hole that had not been there before. I remember the dark, green water closing over my head. My eyes were open, and I saw the water above me. I did not panic. I did not flail with my arms or kick my feet. I had a calm feeling. Some kind of miracle happened then; it felt like I was led by an unseen hand to just walk out of the hole and onto solid land. I wonder to this day at my calmness and that I did not drown.

The second incident concerns my brother Siegfried when I was ten years old and he was thirteen. There was a rich farmer in Landsberg who owned many acres of land. His fields were just outside of town; it was a ten-minute walk to get there from where we lived. In the fall, there was a large stack of straw in one of the fields. Siegfried and I decided one day to climb over the fence and play in this stack of straw. We were having a great time jumping into it and covering ourselves over to hide from each other.

Suddenly the farmer who owned the land appeared. He was a large man who seemed like a giant to us, and he was angry.

"All right, one of you will get a beating for this. Which one of you will take the beating?"

Even though I was much smaller and younger, I did not hesitate to speak up. "I will take the beating," I said and stepped forward.

The man hit me several times about my head and face, but with his hand open, not doubled into a fist. He then told us not to come back into his fields. We had some fun that day, but I paid the price for it. Siegfried did not thank me for offering to take the beating. Perhaps the words did not come to him of what to say.

I should mention now that the German people are not outwardly affectionate, even in close families. We do not hug and kiss each other or voice expressions of love. I did not realize this was unusual until coming to America where people easily say, "I love you," and show signs of affection.

Siegfried and I did not report this incident to our parents. We would have been punished by our father if he had known. In the fall, we bought straw for our animals from this farmer. We also bought farm produce when we could afford it.

The third memory has to do with the old stone Marien Kirche (Church of Mary) that stood in the center of our city. It had a high tower with a huge bell inside. The bell ringer for the church lived in the apartment building in front of our little house. One day, he invited Siegfried and me to accompany him to the church. We were happy to have this invitation. We went along, entered the church, and followed him up the narrow wooden stairs to the top of the tower. He asked us if we would like to ring the bell. Of course we were excited to do that—the bell could be heard for miles around. My brother and I took hold of the rope and began to pull. It took both of us together to ring the great bell; I was twelve, Siegfried was fifteen. It lifted us right off our feet, and we laughed. We rang it until the sound grew louder and louder, reaching across the town. The clapper just over our heads was hurting our ears, but we were happy.

This was a great experience for us. It left a lasting impression on my mind to this day.

* * *

My parents encouraged us to have music in the home. My mother played the zither, and she also had a lovely soprano voice. One of my favorite memories is of her singing hymns of the Church as she went about her work in the home. She was a good writer too. She was always writing something—stories and poems. She wrote several plays for the Church that were produced and acted out for the members.

We children seemed to have been born with an ear for music. My brother Horst learned to play the piano at church; when he mastered it well enough, he played for the sacrament meetings. When he was about sixteen, he bought for himself a little organ that you pumped with your feet; then he could play for us at home. In our family, we had a wooden flute and several harmonicas that all of us could play. I also had a small accordion.

My father loved music. He played the violin and dreamed of becoming an opera singer. He had a very good baritone voice.

World War I interrupted his life's hope. He was taken into the military and was struck in one lung by a bullet while fighting in Romania. He also contracted malaria, a disease which was then untreatable. Malaria will at times go into remission and then return without warning, causing the patient to have chills, high fevers, and uncontrollable shaking.

As a child, I remember my father lying in bed when one of these attacks came on him. The tremors of his body shook the whole bed. This caused my mother great distress because she could not help his suffering.

My father eventually got work with a construction company as a bricklayer. That was very hard work for him because of the injuries he had suffered in the military. But regardless of his poor health, my father was thankful to have a job at all during those difficult times. Work as a bricklayer soon ruined his delicate hands; they cracked open and bled because he was not given gloves for protection. The rough weather in heat and cold also ruined his voice.

My father was a brave man. I remember when at the top of our street two horses that were pulling a loaded wagon got spooked and began wildly to run this and that way down the street. The man on the wagon could not control them. My father saw the situation and ran out in front of the horses. He grabbed the reins that held them together and yelled for them to stop as he was carried along the street. The horses began to slow down and come under control of the driver. My father was not injured, but he could have been killed.

I also have a memory of my father sitting on a little stool in the kitchen mending shoes for our family, friends, and neighbors. At this time, there were no nails to be had. The steel and iron works were producing military equipment, but there was a company that began making nails from wood. Germany has many oak trees, and this was the wood used for making the tacks that shoemakers had to use. They looked like regular tacks, but they did not last as long as metal ones, so shoes had to be mended more often.

People had to be resourceful in those times in order to survive.

When I was old enough, I carried buckets of coal or potatoes from the cellar up the stairs of the apartment building for older women who could not do this for themselves. In this way I earned a little money to add to our small income.

For many years, my mother cared for a sister in our ward who was bedridden. Every day, Mother went to help her. Mother shopped for this sister and made sure she had food to eat. The woman was a widow, and all of her children were gone. There was no one to help her. She had open sores on her legs that never healed for many years. Mother bathed her, treated her sores, and tried to make her comfortable.

One day when Mother was at this woman's apartment, she said, "Emmchen, please pray for me that the Lord will end my suffering."

My mother took this sister in her arms and prayed for our Father in Heaven to please end the suffering of this good woman. At that very moment, as my mother held her, she passed away. So great was my mother's faith in the Lord that her plea was answered without delay.

Mother was a small woman with a delicate body and a big heart for other people. She once had a serious case of pneumonia and went to a sanitarium for treatment. We children were still young then. The Relief Society president came to our home to care for us. She brought fish and other things to feed us.

CHAPTER TWO

The War Years

When students were twelve years old, they became members of the Hitler Youth Organization. The boys in our family were part of the organization but not official members. You had to buy and wear the uniform in order to be official.

My parents could not afford the brown shirt, black tie, and short black pants. With the uniform came a sidearm: a beautiful dagger with a black ivory handle engraved with a red swastika.

There was a slogan, which was thought of by Hitler himself; it became our gospel by which we must live: "Hard as steel, tough as leather, and fast as a greyhound."

This is how we were raised, girls and boys, even at the elementary school level. The principal of our school was a devoted Nazi. He had lost one arm in the First World War. He dressed with pride in his brown Nazi uniform. One day while he was teaching history, he asked us boys, "Who among you would give his life for the Fuehrer?"

Every boy in the room raised his hand except me. I had been taught by my parents and through the precepts of the Church to be honest always. I could not lie. I expected to be punished, but the principal said nothing. From that day on, he treated me with respect.

He assigned me to stay in his office and answer the telephone while he was teaching his class. I had earned his trust. In return, I got out of the history class and could be lazy for an hour.

The boys of the Youth Group went on hikes together, went camping, learned rifle shooting, how to fly glider planes, ride horses, and other exciting sport activities. When these boys left school, they became part of the German army, which is what all their training had been preparing them for.

In 1939, my father was drafted by the city government to serve as a policeman in the town of Landsberg. Two years later, he was transferred to an area in the north where there was a Russian prison camp. He then became a guard for the war prisoners. He was gone for a month at a time and then was allowed to come home for a weekend.

My father told us a little about his experience with the Russian prisoners. He saw them as fellow human beings. He treated them with respect and was never unkind to them. The prisoners were given only small rations of food. My father knew what it was to always be hungry. Out of pity, he often smuggled potatoes in to them. He could have been shot for this if he were caught, or at the least imprisoned.

One day, he went out on work detail with a group of prisoners whose job it was to unload the ships that came into harbor. My father was standing on the wooden planks that connected the ship to shore; his rifle was under his arm. Somehow he lost his footing and fell overboard. He was the only man guarding the prisoners. Escape is what is always on the mind of any prisoner, but these Russian men whom my father had treated kindly were only concerned for his safety; some went into the water and carried him ashore. His gun was restored to him by a prisoner. He was knocked unconscious by his fall, but none of the men he was responsible for tried to escape.

After war was declared, my father was drafted into the military and sent off to fight. Our family did not hear from him and did not know where he was for a long time.

There was a time during the war when potato bugs were eating up all the vines. The farmer who had punished me came to our school and showed us what potato bugs looked like. It was a dire emergency; if the potatoes did not mature, people in the town would starve. We depended on those potatoes for our lives.

Hundreds of schoolboys were transported to the farms. We descended upon the fields and began killing potato bugs with rocks. When we found a bug, we put it on one rock and smashed it with another. We carried the two rocks with us as we moved down the rows.

In the fall, it was schoolchildren who harvested the potatoes because the adult farm workers were all in the military. School was closed for this essential activity. We picked the potatoes up with wire buckets and dumped them onto a truck.

My brother Horst was drafted in 1942, when he was nineteen—the age when he would have been serving a mission for the Church. Horst was an artist. His dream was to attend a school of art, but our family did not have the money for this. He painted beautiful scenes for the family, and was always sketching and drawing something. He liked working with his hands. He made for Elsa and me a little two-wheeled cart in which he pulled us over fields and meadows to our great enjoyment. Then, much too soon, he had to leave our family and go to war.

He was sent to France and later to Russia to fight in a war we could not win. We heard very little from him. Once he wrote from France—somewhere in a bombed-out town. He told us of going into an old church there. He had thought to have a moment of peace and seclusion for prayer inside the church. He went up to the organ, which was still intact. He began playing some of our Church hymns. He wrote that he felt the peaceful presence of our Heavenly Father. Soon other German soldiers were drawn by the sound of the organ and came to listen. They became immersed in the music and were able to forget for a short time the horror of war: the killing, the fear, the death, and the destruction that were going on just outside the church.

Siegfried, who was three years older than I, was drafted late in 1944. The war was going badly for us. The Russian army was every day coming closer. I well remember the last few minutes of time that I spent with him. He was given permission to come home from his garrison where he was in combat training. He only had a short time to visit before being sent to the Russian front. It was on a Sunday evening; we had attended sacrament meeting and were walking home through the dark streets of our town.

My brother was dressed in his gray uniform. We were singing a well-known popular song about soldiers going to war. He left that same evening. We never saw or heard from him again. The German army did not ever contact us about him.

Siegfried was different from others in the family. He lived his own life always alone. He liked sitting in a corner, where nobody would disturb him, and reading. He studied science and mathematics. He was best in his class but never bragged about it. He never talked to us about his hopes and dreams but kept everything inside.

Later, we found among his papers service achievement awards that he received which he had never showed to us or mentioned. He could have become a great man of science who might have done something good for mankind, but all his hopes and dreams were shattered in the war.

Siegfried was seventeen years old when he left us. We feel

that because we did not hear from him again, he was probably killed soon after while fighting the advancing Red Army.

Then came Christmas 1944. There were three of us left at home: my mother; my sister, Elsa; and I. Mother tried very hard to make this as good a Christmas as possible with the little that we had. We had no money to buy presents and, of course, no money for a tree. She went to the Christmas tree lot and got a broken piece of tree that no one wanted. The owner gave it to her. She brought it home, and we decorated it with a few ornaments and some candles. On Christmas Eve, we lit the candles, which gave off a beautiful glow reflected by the ornaments. We had just started our simple celebration when there was a knock at the door.

Elsa was excited; she thought it might be Santa Claus coming after all to bring us some presents. Mother opened the door. A neighbor who was a member of the Nazi party stood there. He came inside and told us that Horst was dead. He had been killed in action on the Russian front. He was shot in the abdomen and probably bled to death.

Our mother thanked the man for coming to tell us and then closed the door. I think back now to our little family huddled together in shock trying to absorb what we had just heard—that our beloved son and brother had died in a horrible way and would never return to our home. I think of our pitiful-looking tree and how useless it all seemed then. Our mother tried to remain calm in her own grief as she held us to her heart. Being myself a parent now, I wonder at the tears that must have poured from her in secret. But in order to help us bear this terrible grief, she tried in our presence to keep her spirits up.

Our father was gone, and we had not heard from him in a long time; one brother was dead, and the other missing in action. Only my sister and I were left. I was fifteen, and Elsa was twelve. We went everywhere together and became almost inseparable. Wherever I had to go, whatever I had to do, my little sister came along.

When my father knew he was going to be gone for so long as a prison guard, he killed our goat so the family could have some meat. We had no kind of refrigeration. For preservation, the meat was salted and smoked.

Then came the time when we had to kill the chickens and rabbits. I had to do this because my father was not there. I had never in my life killed anything; I had only seen my father do it. I became physically ill over having to do this job, thought of it the night before it was to be done, and wondered how I could do it. I would not let my sister watch. I went up the hill alone and came back with the first dead rabbit. It never got easier for me to do this. I would change off—first a rabbit and then a chicken until they were gone. People were killing dogs for meat. I was glad we did not have a dog. We stopped keeping house pets when there was no food for them.

At the close of 1944, our family's life began to change even more. I did not want to be drafted into the war and leave my mother and sister alone. There was an opportunity for me to become an orderly for the Red Cross. I applied for this job, was accepted, received the necessary training to become a medical orderly, and was given a certificate.

My job then was to meet the trains bringing wounded German soldiers from the Russian front and then transport the wounded to our Army hospitals. These men were in horrible condition. The air was filled with the odor of blood, pus, dead flesh, and gangrene. There were young men with both legs amputated who screamed in pain when we moved them onto stretchers.

It was difficult for a young boy such as I not to vomit or pass out from smelling the odors and seeing the condition of these men. I was always thinking that one of them could be Horst or Siegfried or my father.

I prayed constantly to my Father in Heaven to give me emotional and physical strength to do this job. I often was afraid that I would not be able to bear the weight of the stretcher and might drop a wounded soldier.

Once I had to accompany a busload of German soldiers who had sustained head injuries. They were insane and acted very strange. I was a young boy left alone to care for them. I felt threatened and was afraid of these poor souls. I was glad for the bus driver—and relieved when we reached the hospital.

The orderlies must also care for civilians who were wounded in air raids. Whenever the air raid siren sounded, I had to put on my uniform and report to a certain place where first aid was given.

There were times when American planes flew over our little town. They did not usually drop bombs; there was nothing of consequence in Landsberg. But one evening, just as my family sat down to eat, several planes came over and dropped some bombs. This made a terrible explosion. It was so close that the windows blew out of our house. My mother and sister were terrified. They jumped up, covered their ears, and ran around like blind chickens, screaming and crying. For some reason, I was not afraid. My philosophy was that if the Lord meant me to die, I would die; if it was not my time, then all would be well.

The planes were soon gone; we could hear them in the distance, and they did not return. I remember that we had noodles for supper that night. After being so frightened, my mother and sister had no appetite for food, so I ate all the noodles. When they were calmer, we went out to see the damage that was done. There were huge craters in the middle of our street. No houses had been hit, but the windows were blown out of many houses, including the big apartment building.

At this time there was no commerce of any kind going on, no buying or selling of merchandise. We could not get glass to replace the windows. We hunted for boards and nailed them over the windows. This meant that it was dark inside even during daylight hours. There was no electricity. We used petrol lanterns for light.

Later, men came around with glass and replaced as many windows as they could. We were very glad about that because it added to our suffering to be in the darkness and unable to see what was happening outside.

It now became clear to the German people that nothing could save us from the advancing Red Army, but our government wanted us to believe we could still win the war. The closer we came to the end, the more desperate measures were taken to turn the tide.

Boys even younger than fifteen and old men were forced to take up arms that were too heavy for them to carry. They were taken to the front lines, where they had to stand up against the Russian tanks and an army of well-trained Communist soldiers who were fighting for the glory and honor of their beloved Mother Russia.

Christmas 1945 came. It was our last Christmas as a free people living in a free country; it also was our darkest as a family torn apart by war. Shortly after Christmas, our condition worsened while the enemy came steadily nearer.

Each evening, just before going to bed, I would go outside and listen to the sounds of war coming closer. The heavy guns sounded like rolling thunder in the distance. The eerie sounds that heralded death and destruction made me shiver in dread and horror. I knew what the war was doing to our own soldiers. I was always thinking of our men and boys who had to face the Russians, be slaughtered, and die for a lost cause.

These soldiers were not Nazis who volunteered to fight in the war; they were ordinary Germans forced to fight. If they had refused, they would have been shot.

In these hours while I stood outside in the dark and listened, my heart cried out for my people, for my country, and for everything that was dear to my heart—my religion and our freedom.

At this time there was no electricity, no heat, no running water, and no food. Our local government had left us alone without any instructions or advice on what to do or where to go. Before they left, they blew up the bridges that crossed the Warthe River. From that time on, we were totally isolated; our town was without any visible life, like a ghost town. One could not hear the sound of human or animal voices. The city was covered in a dark, deadly silence except for the distant, muffled sounds of war.

One early morning, I went outside the house to observe the situation. I was alone. There was not another soul in sight. Then I saw in the not-so-far distance on our main street, long columns of army troops. It struck me like lightning. "The dreaded Red Army! The Russians are here! All is lost!" The shock of what I saw paralyzed me at first; then I ran home, yelling to my mother and sister, "The Russians are here!"

Fear gripped our hearts. What then happened can only be described by one word: chaos. There was no order; no rules, no laws, no government. There was only one thing we then could do—try to survive. Everybody had to care for themselves.

At first a few people, then more and more people came out of their hiding places, like hungry rats out of their holes. The faces of the people were pale, showing desperation, horror, and the effects of starvation.

We were frightened by the looks of the first Russians we saw. They came from Mongolia. They had rough, hardened faces with Asian features. Their skin was bronze colored; they had black hair, small narrow eyes, and sharp, outstanding cheekbones.

They came down the streets in little wagons pulled by

small horses that had heavy hair, long manes, and bushy tails. The Russians wore gray fur coats and big fur caps. They caused terror wherever they went. Many homes that had escaped the bombings were burned down. The men plundered the houses and raped young girls and old women.

I watched the progression of burning houses that came closer each day to our own neighborhood. I remember the day when the house and business of our branch president was burned. From our house, I could look down the street and see where he lived and worked. On this day, the Russians set fire to his shoe repair business. I was watching as they did it and felt sorrow for our leader. He was an older man, always good and kind to others. While the business was burning, there was a large explosion because of the glue and other combustible material that was stored there. We never knew what happened to him or his family. Our little branch had become decimated. We could not meet together.

We decided it was no longer safe to stay in our house, so we made the decision to leave and go to a friend's house—a woman who was a member of the Church. Very early one morning, we left, carrying large suitcases with our clothes and most precious belongings.

When we came to the center of town, we saw the ugly signs of recent fighting: dead soldiers, dead civilians, and even some dead horses. My mother, sister, and I were fearful all the way as we walked to our friend's house. However, when we got there my mother could not stay. She did not have a good feeling about it. We left our suitcases and returned home.

A few days later, Elsa and I went back to the house of this good sister to retrieve the suitcases we had left. This was a most frightening experience for Elsa because we had to go through small streets with the houses on both sides engulfed in flames. We also had to pass by Russian soldiers and tanks.

The situation was even worse when we came to the home

of our friend. She was not there. Her house had been taken over by a group of wild and drunken Russians. We crept carefully and quietly down the basement stairs. Above us we could hear the soldiers laughing, shouting, and stamping with their feet. I knew without a doubt what would happen to us if the Russians discovered we were there. We both prayed over and over that we would be safe, that we would not be seen, and that we could return home safely.

It was definitely with the Lord's help that we made it safely home with the two suitcases. Our mother had been beside herself with worry, saying a continuous prayer until she saw us returning. She decided that we must now stay in our home and pray for the Lord's protection.

We were worried about our friend. We did not know what had happened to her, and we could not ask questions like that of anyone. We heard much later that she had somehow escaped to the west but died in a few years.

It was not safe for any female to be seen. Women would powder their faces and hair with flour to look old and sick. My mother also powdered herself in this way.

As I have already mentioned, our small house was located behind a four-story apartment building. I was the only male in our entire neighborhood because all the other boys and men were still fighting around the city of Berlin. I did everything I could to protect the women. I nailed boards over the basement windows and made sure that the big heavy front door was kept locked at all times. I kept the iron key in my pocket.

Unfortunately, the Russians discovered another way to get into our place. They came in from the backyard, over the fence, and then entered the apartment building through the back door. The frightened women in the building came running to us for protection. They felt more secure in our little house.

However, not everyone could escape the killing, raping,

and other horrors. One night, a poor old man came crawling to our house. We found him bleeding on our doorstep. We took him inside and did what we could for him.

One morning, a Russian soldier came into our house, walked into the bedroom, and motioned for Elsa to come in. He put his rifle down, leaning it against a chair, and again motioned for my sister to come in. My mother and I watched in horror, not knowing what to do. I could see and hear my mother praying with terror in her eyes. I concluded that I would grab the soldier's gun and shoot him. No matter what, I would not stay there and let him rape my little sister. Some kind of miracle took place. The man picked up his gun and left the house without saying a word. We felt that, once again, we had been protected by a higher power.

There was one rapist in particular that the women feared. We recognized him by his one hand being bandaged. He was the worst. Whenever I was watching the street and the apartment house and could see him coming, I would run next door to where the Russian commander was housed. I reported the rapist in the hope that an officer in charge would help us. I was sure that the rapist knew about me, who I was, and what I did in trying to protect the women. I feared for my life and always tried to hide from him.

I was working for some Russians at a washroom. My job was to feed the furnace, and it was up to me to find fuel for the fire. I used any furniture I could find, anything that would burn. For my work, I received a loaf of bread, which was a priceless treasure to us in this time of starvation.

One morning when I was on my way to work, I went through a stone passageway to get to the other side of the street. This was a dark, tunnel-like place seldom used by anyone, but it was a shortcut for me. Halfway through the tunnel, I saw a man coming toward me. As he got closer, I saw that it was the dreaded rapist that I had reported to his superior.

I was nearly paralyzed with fear and fright. There was no way to escape from him. We were by then so close that I could touch him.

I thought, *Now he will kill me.*

He reached into his pocket and stretched his hand out toward me—it was filled with sugar cubes! He dropped them into my hand and walked away without a word. For me it was a miracle. I had expected to be killed and instead received a precious gift.

A mean-looking Russian soldier now came every morning to pick me up for work. He would knock at the heavy apartment door with his rifle butt. Hearing this, I leaped from bed, ran to the front door, and let him in. It was the same routine every morning: he came in and said "Rabotti!" which meant, "work!" Soon my family became accustomed to calling him Rabotti. He never took anything from us or threatened us. One morning I asked him to sit down. I then sketched a portrait of him, which he was glad to receive.

Our main goal in life was to survive. We were always foraging for food. One day, my mother, my sister, and I went out in search of something to eat. We went into empty buildings, hoping to find something edible. As we came empty-handed out of one building, we were approached by a Russian soldier on a horse. He shouted, letting us know that we were to go with him, all the while swinging a long leather whip in our direction. He drove us like cattle in front of him; we were scurrying along not knowing what he had in his mind to do.

We came to a fenced camp outside the city. An armed guard at the gate took us inside. My mother removed from her clothing a little package of tobacco that she had hidden away for such an emergency. She offered it to the guard in exchange for our release.

Tobacco was something of great value to the Russians because they could not get it anywhere. The guard let my mother and sister go, but I had to stay. My mother was broken-hearted to go outside the camp and leave me behind.

There were others in the courtyard; in fact, it was quite crowded. I walked around and observed the whole place, thinking only of a way to escape. I found in the fence a single loose board. I pulled it a little sideways, and to my surprise, I realized that the opening was large enough for my slender body to slip through.

I looked for the guards and seeing none, I prayed for the Lord to help me get through the fence quickly and not be seen escaping. I squeezed myself through the opening. In a second, I was on the outside and free. Not far away, I saw a soldier on guard. The camp was surrounded by high grass and weeds; I dropped down into the weeds and crawled away like a snake when the guard was looking the other way. My heart was pounding, but I did not lose my nerve. I kept going until I was out of danger of being caught. When I returned home, we three embraced each other and thanked the Lord for my escape and protection.

This was my first escape, but it would not be my last.

Meanwhile Rabotti was gone, probably transferred. My job at the washroom was also gone. I now was ordered to work at the power plant. I shoveled coal to heat the big furnaces that steamed the generators, which produced electricity; however, only the Russians profited from it, not the German people.

I had never done this kind of hard labor before. I was still a young boy and not yet strong. I was always interested in art. After my eight years of schooling, I obtained work as an apprentice at a photographer's portrait studio. This used an artist's eye and hands but not his back. I was each hour of each day wondering how I could pick up another shovel full of coal.

One day, the Russian commander who was in charge came and took me to a nearby horse stable. Inside there was a very fine animal, which looked like a racehorse. I was ordered by the commander to put the harness on the horse and fasten it to a light carriage.

I had no idea how to do this since I had grown up in the city and had nothing to do with horses. I was in a dangerous situation. The Russians expected Germans to do whatever we were told; if we did not, then we were considered saboteurs. You could be shot for that. Again I prayed for the Lord to help me in knowing how to put the harness on this horse and attach it to the carriage. It was a difficult task, but I managed to get the harness at the right part of the horse and then fastened it in the proper way to the carriage. I breathed a sigh of relief and thanksgiving when this all turned out well.

My new job then was to be a driver for the boss, to take him around the city and wherever he wanted to go. When I drove by the other workers who were shoveling coal, they looked at me with envy. Since I had no experience, this was a learn-as-you-go operation. I had to be very careful to steer the horse without running into anything, especially when I had to drive every day through a narrow gate. Soon, however, I learned all the little tricks, much to the satisfaction of the commander and myself.

CHAPTER THREE

Capture

Spring came, and we had survived the cold, harsh winter without electricity, heat, running water, or much food. Our water came from a nearby well. People stood in line to fill their buckets with this precious element.

The starving people planted seeds and waited for their gardens to give them vegetables, which were so desperately needed.

One morning when I walking to my job, I was suddenly confronted by a Russian officer and two other soldiers; they pointed their guns at me and ordered me to go with them. They took me to other homes where they began arresting young people of my own age, both girls and boys. They had a list of names and addresses for the places where these children lived. The children were taken from the arms of their mothers, who cried and pleaded for them. But it was to no avail; all were wrenched away.

We were taken to a kind of prison in the basement of a large house where it was cold and dark. The only light came from a small door that led outside at the end of a long hallway where the entrance to our prison was. A guard was placed there day and night.

The girls were put into one cell, the boys in another.

There were no toilet facilities, no chairs or beds, no place to lie down. We were treated like animals. The girls were in the cell next to ours. We could see them and talk to them through a small opening in the wall, like a window without glass.

The next morning, after a most dreadful night, the process of interrogation began. When I saw the uniform of the officer in charge, I realized that we were in the hands of the dreaded KGB, the secret police of the Soviet Union.

The three boys with whom I shared a cell were taken first. I could hear the lash of a whip and the boys screaming. This was repeated three times with every boy. As I was listening to this, I was praying, "Please, God, help me to brave when it is my turn."

I was the last one to go in. First, I was asked about my father and his whereabouts and then about my two brothers. I told the interrogator that they were soldiers fighting in the war. I also told them about my brother Horst, who was killed along the Russian front, and about Siegfried, who was fighting somewhere and we did not know his fate—that we had never heard from him, or from my father. The interrogator asked if I was a member of the Hitler Youth organization. I admitted to it, even though I was never an official member.

After the interrogation was finished, I was not beaten as the other boys had been but rather treated with respect. I do not know why I was treated differently unless it was because I did not try to lie. It was no secret, and I was sure the Russians would know it, that every boy and girl at the age of twelve became a member of the Hitler Youth Organization, even without wanting to be.

We were called once during the day for our meal, during which we had to take turns with the other prisoners. We all had to eat from the same bowls and use the same spoons. For the first morning, we were given something like cream of wheat. We were very hungry because we had not eaten the previous day. We ate like hungry wolves, gulping down the food even though it had a very salty taste.

During the rest of the day and night, we experienced terrible thirst but were not given even a sip of water. We were all lying on the cold stone floor groaning and writhing in pain. This is the kind of torture the KGB inflicted on us to achieve their devilish desires.

Later that night the guards came and told the girls that they could go out and bring us some water. While the girls were out there the guards brutally raped each of them. That was the price they paid for bringing us water.

Another torture was not allowing us to go out and relieve ourselves. We suffered such agony over this, walking back and forth in our little cells until we were finally allowed to run outside in the yard where a big hole had been dug. We had to do this very fast. Often we were not given time to pull up our pants. When we ran past the guard, he would kick our behinds and laugh.

To break the monotony of our days and nights and to help soothe our nerves, we often sang folk songs. A guard would come and tell us to stop singing or we would be shot. Then another guard would come and tell us to keep singing. The guards told us that we were all going to be shipped to Siberia.

At night we sometimes heard the shelling and bombing of our city, which would make our basement cells shake. This was the last effort of our army to fight the enemy, but it was hopeless. Our Fuehrer had no regard for the life of his people. He ordered them to fight until the last drop of blood was shed. Senseless lives were sacrificed while Hitler in his fortified bunker planned the suicide of himself, his new wife, and Blondie, his beloved German shepherd. Just the day before, Hitler had married Eva Braun in a small, sobering celebration, in the company of the family of Dr. Joseph Geobbels. Dr.

Geobbels killed his own wife and children and then himself a few days later.

So there we were—a group of young people imprisoned by the Russians for no reason other than being German during a time when our country was at war with the Soviet Union. We listened to the shelling of our city, wondered about the fate of our families, and huddled together for warmth and some small bit of comfort.

In the dark of night, there came a moment I will never forget: a young girl in the cell next to us began to sing "Nearer My God to Thee." One by one, the other girls joined in until the sound became like a choir of angels. Being from a religious family and knowing this hymn very well, it brought such tender feelings to me as cannot be described.

No words could better express the feelings of these frightened, crying young souls as they sang, "Nearer my God to thee, nearer to thee, even if I am depressed because of sorrow and pain, and being threatened, and if this should be my fate, despite pain and worries, nearer my God to thee."

They sang as though they were praying to the Lord, and maybe found some comfort in the last words, "Or if, on joyful wing Cleaving the sky, Sun, Moon, and stars forgot, Upward I fly, Still all my song shall be Nearer, my God to thee, Nearer to thee."

Even today, fifty years later, whenever I hear this hymn, inside I cry out for these innocent, pure young girls who had to suffer such terrible afflictions.

One of my cell mates was Guenther. We knew each other because both of us were medical orderlies for the Red Cross. He was eighteen, three years older than I. When he came back from interrogation, he told me that his driver's license, which identified him as a member of the Hitler Youth Organization, had been taken along with his other personal effects and put on a shelf in the hallway. He was very worried about this driver's license because he had lied about being a member, and the license would prove that he had lied. He begged me to get it for him.

I tried to open our small cell door, which was only locked and closed by a latch on the outside. With my smaller hand and long fingers, I was able to unhook the latch and open the door. I crept very quietly down the hallway toward the shelves. The whole time, I could see the posted guard standing outside by the door with his back to me. I found Guenther's license and, at the same time, the large key to my apartment door.

To have this key back was very important to me. Without it, I would not be able to get into our house in the back of the apartment building. All this time I had carried that key wherever I went. I was the one who made sure the door was locked every night to keep out intruders, but without it, I would be kept outside also.

At this time, I was already thinking of escaping and wondering how it would be possible. I was always thinking of a way to get back home to care for my mother and sister.

When I was back inside the cell with the door once again locked, I handed the license to Guenther, who was very relieved. He tore it into small pieces, chewed it, and then swallowed it.

A few days later a great commotion went on outside. We wondered what was happening. Guards came into our cells and took us outside; they put us into trucks and took us back to our homes. Finally, we saw our mothers again. They were so happy to see their children. Unfortunately, we were not there to be with them; we were there only to say good-bye. We were allowed to get some clothing to take with us and then pushed back into the trucks.

The guards kept shouting, "Daway! Daway!" to let us know we must hurry up. We were forbidden to speak to our mothers. If we tried to speak, the Russians yelled for us to be quiet—don't talk! So we could say nothing. We could not tell where we had been, or what had happened to us, and we did not know what would happen from this point on.

My mother gave me an extra pair of shoes. A neighbor woman brought me a piece of bread, which was precious for her to have and generous to share with me at this time of near starvation.

We were taken back to our cells in the basement. One girl told me that her mother had collapsed when she saw her only child being taken away. We left our heartbroken mothers behind, not knowing if we would ever see them again.

The Russians did not give our mothers any explanation for where we were going or why we were being taken away. So these women were left not knowing the fate of their children. My own mother had lost two sons in the war, and she then had to watch as her last boy was taken away by force.

Shortly after our return, we were all taken out into the yard again. We boys were told to stand up against the back wall. One guard pointed his machine gun at us as though he meant to execute us. The other boys were terrified and shaking with fear, but I was calm—not the least afraid. I knew they were just trying to intimidate us. If the Russians intended to kill us, they could have done it on the first day of our captivity or any time since then. They would not have taken us to our families for extra clothing if they meant for us to die.

This turned out to be the truth. We were herded together and taken to where there were now several trucks filled with people lined up. We were again told to get into the back of the empty truck that was there. These were large trucks. We were pushed together with barely room to stand. I ended up face to face with one of the guards. He grinned at me and pushed the barrel of his machine gun into my face. I grinned back at him and turned away. If I was going to be killed, it might as well be then.

Inside my mind, there were feelings of anxiety and near panic. I was thinking of my mother and sister. What was going to happen to them without a protector? My mother was so fragile, and my sister was just a child. The thought of them alone made me sick to my stomach, but there was nothing I could do. I was a young boy, powerless and impotent against an army of heartless men.

The convoy of trucks then drove out of our town. After being incarcerated in the cold, airless basement, it was good to be out in the spring air with the sun shining on our faces. With the optimism of youth, we had new hope, a feeling of life, and we were all thinking that the worst was behind us. We thought we were being taken to some farms, perhaps to plant crops and do other kinds of farmwork. These good feelings were with us during the whole day and as we drove into the evening.

The trucks made a stop so people could relieve themselves. I saw then that only our truck was filled with young people. In the other truck were older men—those who had been too ill or too old to fight in the war.

I was one of the last to get on the truck, and I was pushed against the tailgate, which was about hip high. The truck started with a jerk. My feet were not yet braced for the movement of the truck. I was thrown backwards out of this very high truck, landing on my back and head, and knocked unconscious. Men picked me up, still shaken and groggy, and stuffed me back into the truck. I was forced to stand on wobbly legs that would barely hold me up, and for some time I was not quite myself.

The trucks did not stop again until the sun went down in the west. Then a terrible shock hit us, overwhelmed us, and smashed all our hope. Our happy feelings were replaced by feelings of horror and deep depression.

Our trucks lined up in front of a large gate. I observed the entire place. There were watchtowers on each corner, big spot-lights, and two fences, one next to the other. The first fence was electric; the other was of tall wooden boards, impossible to climb.

Words cannot describe our feelings. My heart stood still and then skipped a beat. Perhaps others had this same experience. Nobody spoke or whispered, so great was our shock.

We were taken off the trucks after dark and herded like cattle into the camp. The girls were now separated from the boys. During our confinement I had set my eyes on one beautiful girl. We had become friends. Before she was taken away she gave me a quick kiss, and our hands touched each other. This was the first time I had ever been kissed by a girl. I saw her one more time when we were separated by a fence. I gave her a small photograph of myself that I had been allowed to keep.

We boys were made to stand in lines inside a large, empty building. Our personal possessions were taken from us: combs, photographs, even the belts which held up our pants; we had to hold up our pants with our hands. All these items were thrown in one big pile outside the courtyard and burned.

I was the only lucky boy who could keep my belt, the photographs of my beloved family, and the key to our building. I do not know how this came about. Once more I had the feeling that angels were looking out for me.

Late in the night, we were pushed into some barracks that were already filled with prisoners. They were mostly older men who were lying all over the place. The smell of unwashed bodies filled the air, along with the sound of snoring. There was no space for us to lie down and sleep, but we had to some-how make room for ourselves.

When this first terrible night was over, we were assigned to our own barracks. We each had a wooden plank on which we had to sleep, covered only by a dirty blanket. For toilet facilities, we had a primitive latrine in the open courtyard. It was a hole in the ground covered by boards. At night we were locked in and had to use washtubs. We were given assignments to carry these bathtubs, which were filled to the top, outside to be emptied into the large latrine. We had to all take turns with this job. Of all that I had been forced to do up until that time, this was the worst. It took a strong act of will not to retch as I carried and emptied the vile-smelling receptacle.

The next thing that happened was that our heads were all shaved. Then we had to take off all our clothes and throw them into one pile to be washed and deloused. We then were made to take showers to get rid of any lice we might have.

When we came out of the showers, we had to pick our own clothes out of one large pile. It was difficult to find your own underwear among all the others. But I felt sure that I had found my own clothes again, which gave me a feeling of gratitude.

For our meals, we went outside the barracks and stood in line. Every day we got the same things to eat. In the morning, there was a tin cup of hot water and a piece of bread. In the evening after coming back from work, we got very hot soup made of potatoes and grain. We shared one pot of soup with two or three other prisoners. Because the soup was almost scalding hot, it was painful to swallow. But I had to try and keep up with the other fellows or else I would have nothing to eat. Every time was an ordeal. My throat was burning, the tears running down my face, but I had to hurry up and swallow. In that kind of environment, each of us was only thinking of himself.

There was never a moment when I was alone; always I was surrounded by other prisoners and the guards. For prayer, I could only lie in bed and say to the Lord what was in my heart. Even when going about following orders, there was in my heart a prayer for protection and wisdom.

In a concentration camp, there is a daily fight for existence, a continuous struggle for something to eat that will
keep you alive. When you become too tired and weak for the
struggle, you die. With me, my sights were continually set on
escape. I must stay alive because of my mother and sister. I
was alert and watchful for any opportunity that might pres-
ent itself.

In the words of the philosopher Nietzsche: "He who has
a *why* to live for can bear with most any *how*." I believe this to
be especially true for the young in a situation where there does
not seem to be a way out. The young do not easily give up a
dream or an ideal.

The routine was every day the same. We had to go outside to be counted and then receive our breakfast of water and
bread, then our work assignments.

The first few days we worked outside the camp at a stone
quarry. We loaded big wagons with heavy stones; then we had
to push the wagons to other places and unload the stone. This
was a hard job that required all our strength. Normally, horses
or trucks would pull the wagons. It was a kind of punishment
for Germans who were too young or too old to be in uniform.
In this way we also suffered the misfortune of our country
being at war with the Soviet Union. Weak, old men who did
not have the needed strength to pull the wagons were kicked
and beaten by the guards.

We also had to dismount railroad tracks and load them
onto trucks. These were then shipped to Russia. The Russians
took all kinds of machinery from East Germany, anything
they could remove. In this way they plundered the whole
country, even the homes of the people, and sent what they
found to the USSR.

After work, when we were back at camp, we washed as
best we could at a place where small holes were punched in the
pipes and water came out. There was no soap and no towels. It

was impossible to get clean, but most of us tried.

With these conditions, it is no wonder people got sick, especially with dysentery—some died of it. We buried the dead just outside the barracks in their blankets without a service for them.

One evening when we were coming back from work, we saw three German dive bombers flying over the camp. They were the famous JU 87, also called Stukas. Next to our camp was a large Russian anti-aircraft battery where Russian soldiers were being trained. Somebody rang a warning bell. Women soldiers ran out from their bunkers and rushed to the big guns. These guns were mounted on railroad tracks; that was the only way to move such large heavy cannons.

Often when the bell was rung, it was for training, but this time it was real. When the guns began firing, the ground shook. Black billows of smoke went into the air from the shell explosions. Two of the dive bombers turned away, one left, one right. But the middle one could not escape. He was hit, and we saw his plane going down with a tail of black smoke. There was time for this pilot to bail out, but instead he steered his plane directly into the aircraft battery, still carrying bombs under his wings. As he smashed into the earth, a terrible, deafening explosion followed that shook the ground and all the buildings.

I found myself lying on the ground. All around there was chaos. Guards were running, shouting, yelling. The women's camp next to us was badly damaged. All the buildings around us had their windows blown out. Shortly after this, we saw many guards with bandages on their heads. We German prisoners were greatly excited and proud of the man who had decided to steer his plane straight into the Russian camp. But we were careful not to smile or show our pride.

One day, our assignment was to go to the train station and work on some boxcars. These boxcars were usually used for shipping cattle. Our job was to nail wires over any openings in the cars. We also were given straw to throw onto the floor of the boxcars. This was done in a hurried way. We wondered about our strange assignment.

As we were finishing, a large group of Russian civilians were brought to the station under military guard. They were herded like cattle up the ramps and into the empty boxcars. They had been taken captive by their own people and were being shipped to Siberia—for what reason, we did not know.

While I was still working on the cars, I jumped down from a ramp and onto the other side of the tracks. A guard yelled and turned his gun on me. He thought I was one of the prisoners trying to get away. This was a frightening moment for me. I came very close to being sent to Russia along with the others.

Again I prayed to the Lord to help me make the guard understand that I was a *Nemetsky* (German) and not an escaping Russian. He waved me away with his gun, and I was much relieved. Always I was in debt to the Lord for looking out for me.

After the stone quarry and railroad tie work was finished, we had other, easier work to do. From then on, our guards would call out a certain number of men wanted for jobs. Guenther and I were still together. I had not given up thinking of some way to escape from this place without being killed. I told Guenther we would wait for a work assignment outside the camp when it might be possible to escape. One day, the call came that I had been waiting for. Twenty-five men were wanted to work in the fields planting potatoes.

"That's it!" I said to Guenther. "Come on." When we were marked as being out of the camp, I gave a different name from my own. I changed my name from Werner Klein to Hans Wernicke. This was part of my escape plan. By using a wrong name at the gate, I could confuse the guards. This way, Werner Klein never left the camp, and Hans Wernicke did not exist. As we were on our way to the fields, I whispered to Guenther that this is our chance today. Once we were out there, we were not coming back to camp.

Guenther was himself almost like a sack of potatoes. He had no initiative. He relied on me to think of whatever we did, even though he was eighteen and I was fifteen. It was up to me to plan our escape in every detail.

As we worked side by side planting potatoes, I talked with Guenther and explained what we would do. I made it very clear to him that we had to do it that day. We did not know if we would get another chance to work outside the camp.

There were three guards watching over us: two walking and one riding a horse. The man on the horse was replaced during the day by another guard, who was also walking. This gave me more hope about being able to escape.

It was almost quitting time. I told Guenther to slow down and stay farther behind the other prisoners. The guards called out the end of work. The prisoners put down their sacks with the seed potatoes and assembled in the middle of the field. All the while, I was watching the guards as we stayed behind. They paid no attention to us: two young boys intent on finishing their work.

CHAPTER FOUR

Escape

Then came the moment—the right time. I whispered to Guenther, "Now!"

We dropped on our stomachs and crawled down the field, which ended in a large ditch that was overgrown with thorn bushes and sticky weeds. We reached the ditch and ran, stumbling and jumping through it. The thorns ripped at our clothing, holding us back. When we reached the protection of the nearby forest, we felt safer.

At the same time, the guards discovered our absence and realized we were escaping. They blew the alarm while running down the field and shooting at us. We ran for our lives. We could run much faster than the guards with their heavy gear weighing them down. The shouting became less frequent until it stopped completely. The silence that followed proved to us that the guards had given up the chase.

This was one of the happiest moments of my life. I hugged Guenther, and we both jumped and shouted for joy. "We are free! We made it! We are free, free, free!"

The feeling we had was so wonderful, it cannot be described. Only a few hours before, we had been prisoners of the KGB, living under inhuman conditions and surely destined for Siberia. We could not really believe that we had managed to escape. No more hard labor, no more filth, no more sleeping on a hard board, no more stinking barracks. We could now breathe fresh, clean air.

This wonderful feeling of freedom burst like a soap bubble almost as soon as it began. We saw other groups of German prisoners, who, like us, were working in the fields. We realized that what we had thought was freedom was fragile and yet to be gained. We returned quickly to reality. We were surrounded by Russians and could be captured again at any time.

From that moment, we carefully watched for Russians. As we moved on, it was late in the day and becoming dark. We continued to walk through the forest, where we felt safer, rather than out in the open.

We came to our first large obstacle: a wide canal of deep, fast-moving water. There was no end of it in sight. We had to cross the water. I found a small dead tree; we pushed it down, pulled it out of the ground, laid it across the canal, and used it to walk across on. I made it to the other side and waited for Guenther to follow. He was afraid and needed a lot of encouragement to even try. Finally, he stepped out on the tree and came across.

Just before night, we found an old barn in a field where we could take shelter and get the rest we so desperately needed. Guenther immediately went to sleep in a corner and was soon snoring. I was much too nervous and freezing cold for sleep. My nerves were on edge also from fear of being discovered. I closed my eyes, but sleep would not come. I lay there and waited for the night to pass. Suddenly, I heard creeping footsteps outside the barn. I was instantly alert, thinking it was our captors still looking for us. My heart pounded so strong and loud into my throat that I was sure anyone outside could hear it. All the time Guenther was sleeping like a baby.

In a few moments, the steps were gone, and all was quiet

again. But for me, sleep was not possible. I gave thanks to the Lord that we had escaped and prayed that He would keep His eye on us as we tried to get home to Landsberg.

When morning came, I felt relieved to have survived the night, and I welcomed a new day. I woke Guenther, and we stepped outside. After a short time of walking, we met an old woman and asked her where we were and if she knew in what direction the Warthe River was. To our great surprise, she told us that we were on our way back to Schwiebus—the place we had come from, where the Russian concentration camp was located. This woman was sent from heaven to save us from making a terrible mistake. I later learned that it is the nature of man, when walking a long distance without any direction, to go in a circle without realizing it.

From then on, we took direction from the sun, railroad tracks, and later the Warthe River, which goes all the way back to Landsberg. Guenther had no ideas of his own; he simply followed whatever I told him to do.

On our way west, we often came across Russian army units and had to hide in tall grass or brush, sometimes only a few feet away from the soldiers.

One evening, we came to a village where we hoped to find a place to sleep. But this village was like a ghost town. There was no light anywhere, no sound of humans or animals, and no movement. We had an eerie feeling about this place of silence and death. We could have gone into any empty, deserted house and stayed there, but we decided to move on.

We later came to a town that was completely destroyed by war. We saw only rubble, shattered shards of glass, burned and blown-up houses. We heard the sound of vehicles and saw coming toward us a long line of Russian tanks and trucks.

They were rolling and rumbling down the narrow street that we walked on. We had only seconds to hide behind a piece of wall barely large enough to cover us.

We had to stay there, pressed against the wall, until the troops passed by. We came out trembling with relief that we had not been discovered. We continued on our way and saw the bodies of dead German soldiers lying where they had fallen and beginning to rot. It was such a pitiful sight to see: these corpses decaying with no one to take care of the bodies, knowing that somewhere mothers and wives waited for them to return home.

One night we stayed in the basement of a bombed-out house where we found a few raw potatoes to eat. Just a few hours before, we had crossed a river with our heavy woolen coats on. Now, with our soaked clothes, we were lying on a pile of wet potatoes, shaking and freezing. Guenther, like always, fell asleep a few minutes after we lay down. I had to listen to his snoring while I lay awake, shivering with the cold and waiting for another terrible night to pass.

When daybreak came we continued on. In a few hours, we came to a small, empty farmhouse in the middle of a large field. We searched the house looking for food. We were lucky to find a brown paper bag with some oats in it. We stuffed the flakes into our mouths, even though they were old and stale.

When we stepped outside the house we were confronted by a Russian lieutenant, a young boy who was the son of the officer, and two soldiers. We were surprised, shocked, and fearful that this was the end of our freedom. The lieutenant thought we were German soldiers. They raised their guns, and we raised our arms in an act of surrender.

The lieutenant wanted to know where the others were. They became very angry because I only answered, "Ja ne panemaju," which meant, "I don't understand."

The lieutenant hit us in our faces with his fist and told me to take off my shoes. He took them from me and told Guenther to take off one shoe. I was told to put on Guenther's shoe. His shoe was much too small, but I knew I had to get my foot in it, or I would anger the Russian even more. Then the soldiers motioned for us to go, which we did, running as fast as we could, each of us wearing one shoe. The soldiers began shooting at us. I could hear and feel the draft from bullets near my ears.

We were running with our arms still raised and the bullets whizzing past us. Guenther then began to scream, "Oh, my God! Please help us!"

Even as I ran—wearing one of Guenther's too-small shoes and terrified of our predicament—my mind registered surprise to hear Guenther calling on the Lord for help. He had told me while we were in the concentration camp that he did not believe in God. I found it interesting to see the outburst from his soul, to call on a higher power when the threat of death seemed to be imminent. So Guenther, in the depths of his soul, did believe in God.

To this day, I do not know if the Russians meant to kill us or only to scare us, but once again I felt that we were protected. If they meant to kill us, they were poor marksmen.

I gave Guenther his shoe that I had been forced to wear. He now had shoes, but I had to continue our journey with bare feet.

Another day came and we were walking along a dusty road through some barren fields that were flat like a table. The sun was hot, and we were tired. There was no sign of life anywhere. We came upon a lonely Russian soldier who was sitting on the side of the road. He was part of a communication unit. His job was to install telephone lines across the land. He was friendly and invited us to sit with him, so we joined him under the shade of a small tree.

We began a conversation and found that he had been a teacher before the war. He could speak and understand some German. He told us that he hated communism and the government in power. He was happy to have someone to talk to. He showed us pictures of his family and told us that he missed his loved ones.

Before we left this lonely man, we asked him if he would write on a piece of paper that we had come back from Russia, where we had been delivering horses. Many Germans were forced by the Russians to bring horses into Russia. They had to walk all the way and then walk back again to Germany. The soldier was willing to do this. He wrote with a pencil on a piece of paper.

We took the paper and departed as friends. With this important piece of paper in my pocket, I was thinking that no one could keep us anymore. When we got to the next village, we walked right through it in the middle of the street. In the past, we would not have done such a thing. However, we now had a sense of security, we felt confident and protected without fear of being arrested again.

When we reached the center of the village, we came upon some Russian soldiers. They stopped us and told us to stay. Then they came over and took us inside a house to the office of their commanding officer. Without saying anything, I handed him the paper. He glanced at the paper and tore it up. We later learned that without a stamp, any document was worthless. No matter what kind of stamp was on it, it would look official, and that was all that mattered.

A guard then took us to an empty room and locked us up. There we were again, captured, our freedom lost because I had been so naïve. The place where we were was a farm with horses, cows, and various kinds of small animals. We were put to work cleaning the stalls and feeding the horses. I was still barefoot. The Russians gave me a pair of tennis shoes with rubber soles to wear.

We had to get up at daybreak and work until evening. We worked with another young German soldier who had been captured. He told us that the Russians had promised sometime ago that they would set him free, but they had not kept their word.

I was not the kind of guy who would be waiting for a release from the Russians. From the first day I was thinking of how we could escape. But actually, our capture this time was a good thing. Today I consider it a blessing from the Lord. We were tired, worn out, and starving when we went to work there. On the farm we had plenty of good food and a straw mattress to sleep on.

We began to hide pieces of bread when we could. We could not go anywhere without a guard constantly watching us. But I discovered that early in the morning the guard would begin to doze off. He was tired because he must start very early also.

One morning, I suggested to Guenther that we should now make a run for it. For this reason we walked behind the barn, but the guard must have been suspicious because he followed us. When I saw him, I quickly took down my pants like I was going to do something there. Since there was no other place for us to relieve ourselves, it seemed natural to him, and he relaxed. He told us to go back to work, which we did. I was thankful for my quick thinking, which probably saved us from a beating.

Two days later, our pockets stuffed with bread, we tried the same thing again. This time the guard paid no attention to us. We used the old barn as a cover, and away we ran—free again.

After a long while, we came to the Warthe River, which would lead us home—except there was one large problem. We must cross the river. Swimming was out of the question; during early springtime, the current was strong, and our heavy winter clothes would pull us down. If we took them off, we would freeze. We had to look for a bridge.

As we walked, we saw a newly constructed bridge built

by the Russian Army Corps of Engineers. It was not far in the distance. But I knew it would be guarded. If we tried to cross, we would be arrested again. I thought of a plan to try and cross very early in the morning while the guards slept. We came to the ruin of an empty house where we might rest for a few hours. Once again, I waited for the night to pass and for the first faint light of day. Guenther was sleeping and not worrying about anything.

The time had come. I stepped outside. Everything was quiet, and a foggy mist hung over the area like a veil. It was perfect: the right moment for us to cross the bridge without being seen. I was anxious to carry out our plan. I went inside to wake Guenther. I shook him awake and told him that we must go now.

To my surprise and dismay, Guenther had no intention to go. He did not want to wake up. I tried to convince him that this was a perfect time. He made no effort to stand. I was disgusted and annoyed with him. I left and began walking but decided to give him another chance and retraced my steps. Perhaps he would think better now and decide to come. But he was still lying there. He told me all he wanted was to sleep. I left him where he was.

I had no choice. He gave up, even though we had nearly reached our goal. After all we had been through together, I hated to leave him. But I had to go on and care for myself alone now.

I never saw him again. I do not know what happened to him. Sometime later, I thought I saw Guenther in the back of an open truck with some Russians, but I could not be sure.

CHAPTER FIVE _____

Alone

By then, too much time had passed for me to try to cross the bridge. I walked along the river looking for a way to get to the other side. Then I saw a horse grazing in a nearby field. I thought if I caught the horse, I could force it into the water some place down river and get across in that way.

Each time I got close, the horse would shy away. I gave up attempting to catch it and kept walking along the river. A few hours later, I found a small boat with one paddle, lying abandoned on the bank. It was old and battered; the wood was rotten, but the floorboards seemed to be intact. I pulled it down to the water and got in. I prayed it would not break apart before I got to the other side. It began to leak almost immediately. I paddled as fast as I could, first one side and then the other, and kept praying for the boat to get me across the river. Just as I touched land, the boat began sinking under me. I scrambled to get out of the water and climb up the bank.

Now I was exultant. I was on the right side of the river to reach Landsberg. After all I had been through, I thought nothing could stop me from reaching my goal. My thoughts were of my mother and sister; a clean, soft bed to sleep in— home was so close now. I was daydreaming like this when I was brought back to reality by the sound of a gunshot.

I looked about. The shot had come from the other side of the river, where a group of soldiers were sitting around a campfire. They were Russians wearing German army coats. One soldier waved for me to come over. He got in a boat, crossed the river, and took me back to his comrades.

One Russian asked where I came from and was I Polish, to which I answered, "Da!" He wanted to know where I was going. I told him I was going to Landsberg where my mother lived. All our speech was in Russian, which I could fortunately understand. At this critical moment it saved me again.

The Russians then invited me to share their food. They gave me a bowl of porridge, which was cooked in a big pot over an open fire. They even offered me tobacco rolled in a piece of their newspaper *Prawda*, which I thanked them for but did not take. I told them in Russian that I did not smoke. While I was sitting there close to the fire, I felt a sharp pain in the bottom of my feet. I was still wearing the rubber tennis shoes that I had been given at the farm, and they were beginning to melt. I stood up, thanked the soldiers, and said, "Spaziba, doswidanja!" (Thank you, good-bye!) I left calmly, not to arouse suspicion, but inside I was nervous and frightened.

So here I was on the wrong side of the river again. I walked until I saw another newly constructed bridge. I did not see anyone guarding it and decided to chance going across. I got to the middle of the bridge before I was stopped by a man in civilian clothes who carried a rifle and wore a red and white arm band.

To my horror I realized that this man was a member of the Polish militia. This was a big shock to me. I thought, *Now all is lost, I will be arrested again.*

We Germans feared the Polish more than the Russians, and the Polish hated the Germans because we were the first invaders of their country. However, the Polish hated the Russians even more than they hated us because they had been oppressed by the Russians for more than a century.

The guard took me to his commanding officer. The officer questioned me in front of the other guards. I told the story that I had made up about taking horses into Russia and now coming back home, but the men did not believe me. I then realized I could not get away with lying to them.

I was so near home after all my troubles, but now it seemed I would not make it after all. To my great surprise, after all I had been through without breaking down, I began to cry. As tears ran down my cheeks I told the real story: escaping from the Russian concentration camp at Schwiebus and the different times I had been recaptured and escaped from Russian soldiers. (I did not tell them about Guenther, for his own protection. I did not want them to search for him.)

The men changed completely. They started laughing, patting my back, shaking my hands, and even congratulating me for being able to get away from the Russians so many times. What a great relief this was to me. They let me go. I was free again. I continued walking across the bridge. Another guard stopped me and took me back to where I had just come from, but the men waved to the guard and told him to let me go.

When I walked onto land, an old German woman was standing beside the bridge. She had witnessed the whole event of me and the Polish militia. She could not believe they had let me go. She said that the Polish guards had arrested many German men and boys and kept them in a large prison complex, where they were beaten and tortured so badly that she could hear them screaming.

She invited me to her humble little home, where she prepared a meal just for me. I remember to this day that there was a fresh boiled egg, some potatoes, and a green salad. Her kindness was so much appreciated—it was the first I had known since being taken from my home. In that time of need, she was like an angel.

With renewed strength and determination, I thanked my hostess and went on my way again, each step taking me closer to home.

As I was walking along the road, some Russian soldiers in a horse-drawn wagon passed by, going in the same direction. I ran after the wagon, and the men motioned for me to jump on, which I happily did. They told me they were on their way to Berlin, where some fighting was still going on. When it got dark, the Russians stopped at an abandoned house and stayed there for a few hours to rest and eat. Then they left me. I had to start walking again, but I was grateful for their help.

The next morning, I beheld a wonderful sight! I saw in the distance the bell tower of the Marien Kirche, our town's great old church. It had stood through the war. I remembered the happy day when my brother and I had rung the bell in the tower. How glad I was to know I was so near home. But the closer I got, the more nervous I became. I knew I could be arrested at any time by the Russians who now occupied our city. I had no papers, nothing to say who I was.

I would not be safe until I was inside our big apartment building, but I also knew that I could be taken away even in front of the house.

I finally entered the city, which now looked so different to me. There were many changes, one being that the big park in our neighborhood was now a cemetery for the Russians.

Home

Then came the moment I had been waiting for so long. I approached our apartment house and took the key from my pocket—the same key the KGB had taken away and I had stolen back. Through everything, I had kept the key. It was very important to me; without it, I could not enter the house. Pounding at the heavy oak door would certainly arouse suspicion from the Russians.

My key opened the big door. I closed it behind me and walked out the back door, where I saw that our home was still standing. It had not been burned like so many of the others. I went inside, opened the hall door, and there in the kitchen stood my mother. She saw me and drew back. She was afraid that I was a stranger who had walked into her house. I spoke to her, and she recognized my voice.

Then we hugged each other and cried for joy. My sister came, and we all embraced. Word of my return spread very quickly. The first woman to come running was the one who gave me that piece of bread when the Russians took me away. She said over and over again, "Frau Klein, I told you Werner would come back."

Later, alone with my family, we knelt in prayer to thank the Lord, who brought us back together and who protected me so often, especially when my life was in jeopardy.

My reason for getting home was to be a support and help to my mother and sister. When I was away from them, I was always fearful about how they were surviving with no man to care for them. I must be a protector of our little family, even though I was only a boy of fifteen.

While I was gone there had been no word about our father or Siegfried.

I needed a bath and clean clothes. I sat down to unlace and take off my tennis shoes. I then realized that the rubber of the soles had melted into my skin when I sat at the Russian campfire. But the shoes had to be removed. Despite the pain, I pulled them off.

Blood flowed from the bottoms of my feet. My skin was imprinted with the pattern of the shoe soles. I had walked from the concentration camp at Schiebus, ninety miles or more, all the way home to Landsberg, but I could go no farther. For me, this too was a miracle.

My mother bandaged my feet. Then I was able to sleep in a soft, clean, white-down feather bed, something I had dreamed about since my capture. I will never forget this first night after returning home. It was like heaven; for the first time since my escape, I could close my eyes and finally sleep without fear of the enemy coming upon me. I had actually had no real sleep since our escape, only in dozing naps when I was trying to stay awake from fear of being set upon by the Russians.

When I awoke the next morning, the sun was shining through the windows. I lay there enjoying being alive, being home, together once again with my family. I was still just a kid, but I felt older somehow. I was not the same boy who had been taken away.

Much of what had happened during the past months had been terrifying. Prisoners in concentration camps walk hand in hand with death each moment of their captivity. They dream of freedom, knowing that they may not survive, always fearing death in that ugly place. Old men know that unless the war ends soon, they will die, and there will be nothing to mark the place where their body was thrown away.

But here I was, one of the lucky ones who got away. It was hard to realize that I had actually escaped captivity time and again, and somehow—miracle of miracles—I was free.

Then I thought of my comrades who were still imprisoned. I knew that things would have been harder for them because Guenther and I had escaped. I felt guilty over that.

For a few days, I felt like I was waking from a terrible nightmare. I was sleepwalking for a while, trying to wake up and deal with a new reality that I could not quite grasp. Day by day, I gradually came to grips with my new situation. Then I had to face the fact that I was not completely free. We were still surrounded by the enemy. The Russians could come at any time and take me prisoner again.

Whenever we heard a banging on the apartment door, I jumped out the back window of our house, went over a nearby fence, and hid in a neighbor's yard. We lived in constant fear until I became better adjusted. The time came when I was able to free myself of this terrible paranoia. I was able to convince myself that the Russians, so far away in Schiebus, had lost interest in the escape of a young, unimportant German boy.

We carried on with our daily lives as everyone around us was doing despite the hardships brought about by the war. It was some time before I could wear shoes and walk normally again.

Then came the day all the world had been praying for: peace was declared.

The bloodshed ended, the killing and fighting stopped: Germany surrendered. It was May 10, 1945. I was now sixteen years old.

Werner's illustration of a quiet place in the Spree River where baptisms were held in Cottbus.

*Werner and Elsa, best friends
since childhood, 1950.*

City of Cottbus, East Germany, 1948.

*Front of apartment building with the
heavy oak door taken away and replaced
by inexpensive wood in 1984.*

*Wartburg Fortress, where
Martin Luther was held hostage.*

Werner, clowning for the tuberculosis ward in the hospital.

Marien Kirche (1984), which escaped the bombings of two World Wars.

"Seigfried and I rang the ball in the tower until the sound grew louder and louder, reaching across the town."

Missionaries in the city center at Eisenach.

Missionaries going up the mountain at Wartburg.

The Warhne River, 1984.

*In Prague, the circus people are welcomed by
the mayor. Epi Vidane has announced "no alkol for Werner." He is
served orange juice instead.*

Werner and his friend, Gitta the elephant.

*Elephants on parade, Jenny on the left, and Epi Vidane announcing,
"The Circus Busch is in town. Come one, come all to the circus."
Werner is riding Gitta on the right.*

Werner playing the organ for Church services.

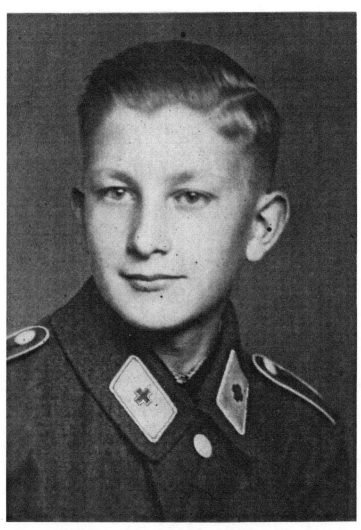

*Werner, age fourteen, medical orderly
for the International Red Cross.*

Werner being released from the hospital in 1948.

Leaving on his mission in 1958.

Werner's parents, Emma and Emil Klein,
circa 1948 in Cottbus, East Germany.

Emma Klein, circa 1971.
"My mother was always writing something."

Linda Trinny and Werner on their happiest of days after being married on January 8, 1971.

Award-winning painting.

Werner's award-winning painting
Come, Come Ye Saints.

"Moresch," the menacing Hungarian steer that required twelve men to move him from place to place.

Circus animals.

This painting won first prize in an Intermountain Art Society show and was selected by the Utah Arts Council from several hundred entries for a traveling show throughout Utah.

"Mohatsch," the circus horse.

Tiger.

Wolf.

Peace

For us, the peace that followed was worse than the war. There was no communication between the German and the Russian government. It was much later that we learned of the surrender of Germany.

As a result of the Potsdam agreement, Germany was divided into four parts. East and West Prussia, the richest and best parts of Germany, were given to Russia. From there to the Oder-Neisse River, the country was taken over by the Polish government. The Western part of Germany was controlled by the other three powers: France, Great Britain, and the USA. Berlin, the capital city, was also divided.

People in West Germany began a life of peace, leading normal lives as they had done before the war. But it was very different in East Germany, where people suffered even more because of starvation, suppression, oppression, and all kinds of inhumanities.

The first my family knew of the changes was one morning when Polish soldiers came into our house and ordered us to leave. We had fifteen minutes to pack a few things into three suitcases, which we put in a small hand wagon. All poor people like us were forced to get out of the Mark Brandenburg country. We left behind what we could not carry.

The evacuation order was Poland's first step in destroying the people of East Germany. The Polish government was happy for their spoils of war. It was payback time for them. They did not care what happened to the German people; they only wanted the land. This was our experience with "peace."

We began to walk west with millions of other refugees, not knowing where we should go or where we would end up. No one told us anything, and no one was in charge. We just kept moving, following the others. There was one thing I was grateful for: I had returned home in time to be with my mother and sister during this period of terrible trial.

It was summer. The sun beat down on us, and water was scarce. It was a heartbreaking thing to see the human tragedy—homeless people moving slowly along with what strength they had, tired and weak from the heat and starvation.

One could see mostly women and children with their faces reflecting the depression and horror of the ordeal they were going through. We began to see people breaking down at the side of the road—just lying there because they did not have the strength to take another step. There was no help for these poor souls. We each had to fight our own battle for survival.

We had to move on, leaving these people behind with no one to care for them until death should come and relieve them of their suffering. We saw this every day, and we felt deep agony in our minds and hearts as we passed by and could do nothing to help. The condition of the abandoned people particularly distressed my mother, who had a tender heart and wanted to help those in need. There were always tears in her eyes when she had to turn away and go on.

I discovered among the refugees Kurt Aurig, my old master of photography, a great artist in his craft, and his wife. He had been kind to me when I was apprenticed to him. He had taught me all he knew as I helped him with the work. His studio had been burned down. Only once did I see him after the Russians took over our town. He had been down on his hands and knees, repairing the cobblestone streets. He, like so many others, was forced to do this kind of hard labor as punishment. When I saw him, I felt so sorry for this gentle old teacher who was not used to hard labor. But there he was, lifting and putting heavy stones in place using a big hammer. I thought how this would damage his delicate artistic hands. I feared he would not survive such brutal treatment.

I was glad then to see that my old friend was alive, but now he must walk with his wife to some unknown destination. We were all refugees together. I feared for his wife, who was heavy and had trouble walking.

One evening, we reached the city of Kuestrin, which had been a fortress against the Russian army and was now completely destroyed. We were looking for a place to stay overnight, but there were only remnants of buildings left. While we were there, the feeling came to me that this is where my brother Siegfried died. We never had any proof of this, but I have always believed it.

We spent the night among the ruins. The next morning, we found a train that went west and got on it. We rode for a few hours and then the train stopped in the middle of nowhere. It could go no further, so we had to get off.

The next night, we stopped near a road and lay down in a field to sleep. I saw an abandoned house and went to see if I could find something to eat. I found a small cellophane bag with some clear crystals in it that looked edible. It was growing dark, and I could not see well. I decided to taste what was in the bag. When it touched my tongue, I knew it was something that should not be eaten. It was very bitter. I tried to spit it out, but the crystals dissolved instantly in my mouth. Some ran down my throat with the saliva. I went back to my mother and sister.

A short time later, I became intensely ill. I started vomiting with terrible force, even though there was nothing in my stomach. At the same time, I was struck with diarrhea. In my distress, I made so much noise that some Russian soldiers came to see what was going on.

They pulled me up by my shirt, put a flashlight in my face, and then dropped me. The other refugees next to us were afraid of the Russians and were upset with my family because we had drawn their attention.

The next morning, while the trek moved forward, we had to stay behind because of my condition. Some hours later, we also moved on, but I was too weak to walk. I lay on top of our belongings in the little wagon, which my mother and sister had to take turns pushing and pulling. Later we discovered that the cellophane bag contained rat poison.

From that time we were on our own. The others had long gone. We learned years later that the people from our town went on to the city of Hamburg in northwest Germany. This was in the American sector, where people were saved and cared for by the government. They received assistance in every way to help them live.

We traveled a different road. When we came closer to Berlin, we stopped at a village on the side of the road just to rest. An old man came to us. He took us into his humble home and shared his meager meal. It was our custom to thank the Lord for our food and to ask for His blessings. The man was very moved and impressed by my mother's prayer. He had tears in his eyes when she finished.

When we finally reached the city of Berlin, we were exhausted and hoped we could stay there. But we were turned away and told we must go on. The Red Cross gave us some food, but this is all the city government did for us. We kept walking and pulling our little wagon.

Some days later, we came to a farm that was managed by

Russians. I suggested that we go inside and ask for food and shelter. My mother and sister were afraid. I had a good feeling about it and convinced them to come along, enter the place, and try our luck.

How lucky we were! The Russians needed help on their large farm. There was work we could do. They would feed us and give us a place to stay. We found there everything we needed at that desperate time.

When we were settled, I went to the main building to ask for food. I was given a large chunk of golden, fresh butter and a large piece of bread just from the oven. When I came bearing this treasure, my mother and sister could not believe their eyes.

Oh, how happy and glad we were to kneel and thank the Lord for this food that came to us like manna from heaven. I never tasted anything so good. I felt that the Lord had guided us to this place.

This began a new chapter in our lives. We were vagabonds without a home. We had to work for the Russians, together with other Germans who were in a similar circumstance. We shared one large room with the other German evacuees. There was one thing I did not like: the snoring and other human noises at night. It reminded me too much of the concentration camp.

The food, however, was wonderful. Every day we had potatoes, lamb, bread, and butter; it was almost too rich—our stomachs were not accustomed to such good things.

My mother worked in the fields with other women. My sister and other young girls were assigned to herd sheep. Since I had become experienced as a driver, I was given the job to be chauffeur of a one-horse wagon. I was very lucky to get this easy job, and I liked it. I was quite satisfied with my life on the farm.

I went every few days to the nearby town of Gransee, the

headquarters of the Russian commander, to deliver farm produce. It was pleasant to drive alone through the countryside,
which was very beautiful then, with everything green and
growing. I was full of good health for the first time in many
months. I was my own boss. Nobody told me how to do my
job. But then it happened that other workers, those who had
to work in the fields in the hot sun, began to be jealous of me.
When I drove by in my little horse-wagon they were envious.

One boy in particular was hostile toward me. He had the
feeling that he was better than others. His father came from
Poland and was able to speak Russian. He worked as a trans-
lator for the Russians. One day, this boy and I had to load
fruit onto my wagon, but the boy refused to help. He stood
back and let me do the work. When I confronted him, a fight
ensued between us in which I beat him up quite nicely. This
caused him to be more humble, and he began to work side by
side with me. The women who were working in a nearby field
observed what happened with great satisfaction because this
family had the habit of looking down on all of us.

My easygoing life at the farm began to be threatened by a
Russian man who caused my family great concern. He picked
me out of all the other Germans to hate. I think he saw in me
the personification of a mean, cold-hearted Nazi. He seemed
to have only one thing in mind—he meant to kill me. That
was his goal, and he pursued it with determination.

Whenever this man saw me on the farm, he came at me
with a rifle; several times he shot at me, but I saw him coming
and got away. One time, we met unexpectedly in the foyer of
the big farmhouse that, before the war, belonged to a German
family. At this time, he did not have his rifle. In the hall was a
large oak table with a beautiful Chinese vase on it. He picked
up the vase and hurled it at my head. I ducked away, and he
missed.

I ran from him up the stairs until I came to the attic. I

went inside and hid myself behind some old furniture. He followed and searched for me while I sat with my heart pounding. He was a big fellow. I knew he would beat me to death if he found me. He gave up looking and left. I did not leave my hiding place for some time because I was afraid that the man might be just waiting until I should appear. My mother was very worried when I did not come to our room at the usual time. When I told what had happened, she became even more fearful for my life. She worried and prayed for me constantly and could not be comforted because she knew this man's evil intent.

Her prayers were soon answered. This Russian man was an alcoholic. He was always looking for something to drink. He never came after me when he was drunk, only when he was sober. One day, he drank too much methyl alcohol and died.

I had the honor of driving his coffin with my horse and wagon to the cemetery for burial. What a relief for my mother and sister, but especially for me. We could finally breathe easier and sleep without fear and worry.

While working there at the farm, I fell in love with a fine, young girl. She had lovely blue eyes and blonde hair. It was for us the love of innocence and youth, an experience that can only happen once in a lifetime. Without expressing our feelings, we both felt in our hearts a strong tenderness for each other. Wilhelmina was her name, but she was called Helmy. She was a quiet, shy girl who was herself experiencing first love.

Whenever we could come together and share a few minutes after our work, we did so. Under the circumstances, there was no other way we could meet. Those few minutes were priceless treasures to us. I thought of her so much of the time and always looked forward to our next meeting.

There is a folk song dear to the heart of German people

called "Roslein," which means little rose. Roslein is the symbol for a young girl, and the song is a love story about a boy and girl.

Often when I thought of Helmy, the words of this song, by Johan Wolfgang Goethe, would come into my mind, and I would sing of Roslein.

> *A boy saw a little rose at the meadow, she was young and*
>   *beautiful.*
> *He ran to see her from nearby with great joy,*
> *Roslein red, Roslein at the meadow.*
> *The boy said, "I will break you Roslein at the meadow."*
> *Roslein said, "Then I will prick you so that you always think*
>   *of me, and I will not suffer it."*
> *Roslein red, Roslein at the meadow.*
> *And the wild boy breaks the Roslein at the meadow,*
> *Roslein fought back and pricked him,*
> *And nothing could help him, he had to suffer it.*
> *Roslein red, Roslein at the meadow.*

I had carried art supplies with me from Landsberg. Knowing that Helmy and her mother were Catholic, I painted for them a portrait of Christ wearing the crown of thorns. They were grateful for this gift, and I was happy to bring a bit of pleasure into their life.

Then came the day that shattered my life—the Russian farm manager called all the workers into the courtyard and read from a list. It had the names of those individuals and families that were not needed anymore and had to leave. When the names of our family were read, it hit me hard. It was a terrible and unexpected shock.

I looked at Helmy, who was standing across from me, and saw in her face the pained surprise that I also felt in my heart. She and I were separated without the opportunity to say good-bye. We had to leave that same morning, while the others went to work. I could have run back to see her, but I did not have the strength. I knew it would be a forever good-bye; seeing her again for the last time would have been unbearable.

With a broken heart, I went on my way. I never saw or heard from her again, but even still I do not forget this girl— my first love. I carried her picture with me for a long time.

Again my family and I were on the road not knowing where we would go or where we would find shelter. At the farm, we had worked all summer for what we could eat and a place to sleep, but otherwise we were the same as before, with no money and no place to go. All we owned was in the three suitcases we carried.

Later on that day, we came to a little village named Koenigstett. We stayed there with some farm people. They took us in, not from the goodness of their hearts, but by order of the mayor. We had one simple room for ourselves, but we were grateful to have anything at all.

In this village, there was nothing for my mother and sister to do, but for me there were different jobs. I was put in charge of caring for the bodies of anyone who died. Two local boys were assigned to assist me in burying the dead. We used a small, flat hand-wagon to move the corpses from the place where we picked them up to a field outside of town. The three of us dug a hole and then dropped the bodies in. No one else was there—no city official and no funeral service, no name plate or grave marker.

These were the bodies of refugees who had no family or relatives. This is the way they ended up, forgotten and unknown.

Once we were sent to a little house where an elderly woman had died. When we got to the house, not a living soul was there. The other two boys were afraid to go inside, so I went first and told them to follow me. We went up narrow, small steps to a dark attic room where we had been told the body was. The boys stayed some distance behind. I decided to play a trick on them. I opened the door to the room and cried out, "Oh, no! She's moving." The boys nearly fell down the stairs trying to get away while I stood laughing.

A short time later, I was given another job. Together with some other boys, I was sent to an ammunition plant that was partially blown up. It was located in a nearby forest. The explosion had sheared and shattered many trees just above the ground. Our job was to cut away the remaining stumps so they could be used for firewood.

Like always, there was no one to supervise us. It turned out to be the most dangerous job I ever had. There were a lot of unexploded mines lying around everywhere—in the grass, in the sand, and between the trees. We had to watch every step we took. One wrong step meant a serious injury or even death.

We always walked in a line, one after the other. The mines were only one step away from where we walked. During our breaks, we built a fire and threw in the old rifle ammunition, which would explode. We did not think about the danger. I even picked up phosphor grenades, unscrewed them, and pulled out the little string, which activated the grenades. I knew I had a few seconds before a grenade would explode. I would stick the grenade in my pants pocket and walk around with the smoke from the grenade coming out the little opening, proving that it was still active. I always guessed the time when the grenade would explode. Just before that happened, I would pull it out and throw it away. These phosphor grenades were made to start fires; they would burn even under water and could not be extinguished.

One day, as we were playing around like this, we saw a horse-drawn wagon coming down the street. In the wagon were the bodies of two men who also worked at the ammunition plant and were killed by a mine. During this time, so much had happened to me and to our family that I believe I was in some kind of mental shock; I had become inured to death, pain, and suffering and had no fear of it.

Christmas 1946 came. Our family was in a very sober mood because we had nothing to eat except potatoes. My mother wanted to bake something for us, but she had no flour. The night before Christmas, she decided to go to the flour mill in the hope of getting a little flour for us. It was already late and dark, and a deep blanket of snow covered everything. We tried to keep her from going, but she was determined.

My sister and I were alone. We worried for our mother's safety, alone in the fields in the middle of the night. As time went on and she did not return, my sister could not bear it any longer. She left the house to look for our mother without my knowledge.

Elsa got lost because there were no road signs, only fields of snow as far as one could see. Even the fences were covered. To make matters worse, a middle-aged man in a wagon stopped and asked my sister where she wanted to go. When she told him, he offered to take her there. Gladly she climbed into the wagon. Almost immediately, the man attacked my sister and tried to rape her.

He pulled down her woolen pants, and when Elsa started to scream, he took his hands and began choking her. At that moment, the man would probably have killed my sister, but his horses began rearing up, snorting, and trying to get away. He had to let go of Elsa to calm the horses.

Elsa jumped out of the wagon. She began stumbling around in the snow trying to get her pants pulled up and get away at the same time. The man drove off, but he yelled to her, "I will come back and get you later."

Meanwhile, I had realized my sister was gone. I went outside and began calling her name so she could hear me and find her way home. Elsa ran toward the sound of my voice.

She was completely breathless from running through the deep snow trying to get home before the man came back and found her. She was so frightened that she lost her shoes and did not know it. When I saw her coming, I ran toward her. She fell into my arms sobbing. Tears were freezing on her face. Her eyes were wild with fright.

I took her into the house by the fire, took off her wet clothing, and rubbed her nearly frozen feet. I wanted to know what had happened to her, but she was so incoherent trying to talk between sobs that I could only guess. Then she went into deep shock and was unable to speak for two days.

My mother came home with her treasure: a little sack of flour. But when she heard my story and saw Elsa's condition, she was too concerned to even think of baking a cake. Both of us were terrified for Elsa. We did not know the full story for several days. My mother blamed herself for leaving us to go and look for flour. She herself could have been hurt, or she might have lost her way and become frozen in the snow, all for a bit of flour.

The thought of her young child going out into a cold, barren landscape to look for her and then the thought of what might have happened nearly broke my mother's heart. She began weeping; I tried to console her, but at the same time, I was also frightened and worried about my sister. Once again we knelt to thank the Lord, that despite human foolishness, His eye was upon us. We were safely together.

Mother got into bed with Elsa and wrapped her arms around her trembling body. All night, she slept that way, trying to bring comfort to her traumatized child.

Spring came. We had survived one more winter. My mother was impressed to write a letter to a Latter-day Saint ward that she knew was in Cottbus. She had no address but tried to make contact with the Church anyway. Since the Russians came into Landsberg, we had been without the fellowship of the Saints. We missed this association and the opportunity to partake of the sacrament.

Weeks went by without a reply to my mother's letter. We supposed the Church members had been scattered as we had been or perhaps the letter was lost. We forgot about it and went on with our lives.

We were greatly surprised one day when a young woman came to us. She said she had been sent from the Church at Cottbus in response to our letter. She had come to accompany us there. We were to leave right away. She said there was a surprise waiting for us.

Leaving Koenigstett so suddenly was difficult for Elsa and me. We had finally made some friends and had begun to fit in. At this time, we were involved in a play production that the local people were staging. We both had parts in the play, and I had painted the scenery for the background. We told our mother that we wanted to stay where we were. But she listened to the Spirit, which told her that we must go.

We packed our few belongings once again, and Elsa and I reluctantly left. Along with our broken hearts, we left behind a sack of potatoes that the farmer had given us.

The four of us waited several hours for a train going in our direction. After a long and uncomfortable ride, we arrived at the city of Cottbus, more than a hundred miles by train from Koenigstett. Traveling was tedious because people had to often stand for the entire distance, and the tracks were in such poor condition that the trains could go no more than twenty miles per hour.

CHAPTER EIGHT

Reunion

Finally we arrived and were greeted by Brother Fritz Lehnig, the branch president. President Lehnig was also in charge of a refugee camp that took in members like us who had been forced out of their home and country.

We were taken to the Church headquarters, which was also President Lehnig's home. He invited us into his living room. When we were gathered inside President Lehnig opened the door to the next room and a man walked through. The man had a heavy beard. It was our father—but for several seconds we did not recognize him. We had not heard a word about him since he left for the war; we had not known if he was dead or wounded; or what was his fate might be until that day. My father had been fighting on the Western front since he went into the war. The enemy he fought was the Americans. He was captured and taken prisoner by them. When Germany surrendered, he was released. That was when he found his way to Cottbus.

Like us, our father had remembered there was a ward in Cottbus, and he went there, guided by the Spirit of the Lord. This was a wonderful surprise for all of us and was the reason why the sister who came for us was so insistent that we accompany her. After all we had been through, we were together again as a family. What a relief it was to turn the burden of being the man in charge over to my father.

For a while, we lived in the refugee camp where we found shelter, food, and member friends. A few weeks later, we were able to get a tiny apartment, which was not much, but we were grateful for even the smallest blessing. We still had to face the biggest problem: lack of food. Everyone was on the edge of starvation. There was no place to buy anything, even if money was available. Nothing was for sale.

At night, we went out on the streets and searched in garbage cans for anything edible, like potato peelings; if we were lucky enough to find some, we cooked and ate them. We began to think of the sack of potatoes we had left in the village of Koenigstett. My father decided that Elsa and I should go back to the village and retrieve the potatoes.

Traveling by train at this time was not only dangerous but also often impossible. There were never enough trains, nor was there enough room for all the people who needed transportation. Many railroad tracks were destroyed; others were removed and taken away by the Russians. The trains also would go unscheduled, traveling whenever they had enough fuel for steam. People would sit on the cold, hard ground, freezing while waiting for a train to arrive, which always took hours.

It was wintertime again when Elsa and I left home and went to wait for a train. When the train finally came, people rushed toward it. They stormed the cars, pushing and fighting for a place. Those who could not find room climbed on top of the cars, or they would stand on the foot boards outside, holding onto the iron railing.

With luck, Elsa and I found standing room inside a car and were on our way to Koenigstett. There we found our sack of potatoes. We stayed overnight, sleeping in the barn. The next morning, I baked us some potatoes in a small stove. Later that day we had to return to Cottbus. But our situation was quite different than before. Now we each had a heavy box of potatoes to carry. The cardboard boxes were held together with wire, and the wire cut into our hands. We did not have gloves to protect our hands from the wires or the cold.

When the train came we were not as lucky as we had been on the way to Koenigstett. We could not get a place inside the cars. The boxes hampered us from moving quickly. We had to travel by standing outside on the narrow boarding platform. With one hand, we held the potatoes. With the other hand, we had to hold the iron rail; otherwise, or we could be thrown from the train.

Night came. The weather was very cold, and it had begun to snow. We endured our miserable condition: no gloves, no caps, with the falling snow blowing in our faces.

In Berlin, the train stopped. We then had to walk to another train station. The city was completely destroyed from the war. We could find no shelter. The boxes became heavier each step we took. Elsa's box weighed the same as mine, about twenty-five pounds.

We two children were alone in the middle of the night, surrounded by Russians and the ruins of a terrible war that had destroyed our country. We were hungry; we had eaten nothing since the baked potatoes that morning.

Elsa was by now physically and emotionally worn out; she was cold and tired, and she did not want to go through this anymore. Her hands were cut through by the wires around the boxes.

I felt sorry for my sister. We were in a bad situation. I told her that we had no choice. We had to go on. We prayed together for the strength to endure what we must until we reached our destination. She then picked up her box again and followed me.

We arrived at the other train station and waited hours

in the cold for a train to come. When finally the train came, everything was as before—every man for himself getting on the train. We two kids were pushed and shoved and had no chance to get inside a car where we could be warmer. Once more we had to stand outside with the cold wind blowing against us. It felt sometimes as if the wind was blowing a hole through us. Unless we froze solid, it was not possible for us to be colder than we were. It was only our youth and the Lord's blessing that kept us alive.

At one time, I fell from the moving train, landing on my knee and cutting a hole in my pants. Fortunately, the train was moving slowly. I was able to run and jump back on. Elsa was terrified when she saw me fall, not knowing how badly I was hurt, or if I could get up and come back. She thought she was left alone with two boxes of potatoes and no brother to help her.

We did finally get back to Cottbus with the precious load of potatoes for which we had risked our lives. When we arrived home, our frozen hands were cut deeply and bleeding from the thin wire of the heavy boxes.

* * *

Slowly life in East Germany began to normalize. My father got work doing construction. My mother spent most of her time trying to find food for us. She and an LDS sister put rucksacks on their backs and went by train to nearby villages where they would go to the farmers and ask for farm produce. While doing this, they saw a need the farm women had for someone to mend their aluminum pots and pans. It was not possible to buy new ones; there were none on the market, and if there had been, no one could have afforded them.

A company in Cottbus had started selling kits for mending pots and pans. In the kit were small squares of aluminum and some glue to affix the squares to a leaky spot. The two women bought some of these mending kits and went out to the farms, where they bargained for food by fixing the housewife's cooking utensils. In later years, my mother joked to us that they did not go to the same farmer twice because they did not really know if the aluminum piece they fastened on with the glue would hold. They made sure to go to a different place each time.

Elsa found work in a factory. I was lucky to find a job working at a photo lab and portrait studio. Our customers were mostly Russian. The reason we could be in business was because we got our photo supplies from the Russian commander, who was in charge of the whole city.

I was always interested in art. I spent many hours sketching and drawing things that interested me. When I was seventeen years old, it was announced from the Church pulpit in Cottbus, that an art contest was being held in commemoration of the one-hundredth anniversary of the pioneers reaching the Salt Lake Valley.

I did a large watercolor poster showing a handcart company in the foreground, Brigham Young as the dominant figure at the center, and the beautiful Salt Lake Temple in the upper background.

We always had our big Church conferences in Dresden. In July of that year, the Saints gathered from all over East Germany for the Pioneer Days celebration. It was a three-day event. We slept on beds of straw. We had many kinds of youth activities. Each branch and ward had been given dances to learn. Several hundred young people gathered at the center to perform these dances. It was a great opportunity for the German young people to meet and get to know each other.

A wonderful thing happened for me at this conference: my painting won first prize. The prize was a small Hershey candy bar. This does not sound like much of a prize now, but in East Germany, there was no chocolate then, so it was a big treat for me. I think that all those who entered the contest got the same prize. The prizes were awarded by our mission president, Brother Walter Stover, who managed somehow to get these Hershey bars for us. He later immigrated to Utah and became a prominent businessman in Salt Lake City. He always gave work to people who came to America from East Germany.

Then came the day that changed my life drastically. One early evening, when I was eighteen years old, a friend and I decided to visit a girl we both liked. We took my friend's bicycle. I was at the front, and he was riding on the rack in back. We were laughing and yelling and having a good time.

As we came closer to the girl's apartment house, we had to ride through a little park that was on one corner of the street. There, out of nowhere, appeared a Russian soldier, also on a bicycle. In a split second, we crashed into each other. I really don't know how it happened. The impact hit me so hard that I lost consciousness. When I came to my senses, I was lying on the ground bleeding. I thought I must have been hit in the face by some part of the other bicycle. My friend ran to the nearby apartment house, and an ambulance was called. The Russian who had hit us just disappeared.

The next day, I looked in the mirror and saw what looked like a grotesque mask. My nose was broken in two places, the bridge completely pushed inward. My entire face was swollen, my eyes almost closed. It was an indescribable shock to see such a drastic change in the way I looked.

The next day, a doctor operated on me. He did what he could to fix the broken bones, but the bridge was severely damaged and could not be the same as before. When I came home from the hospital, no one recognized me, not even my own family. Some years later, I had three more operations, two of them cosmetic. Even after the surgeries, I do not look on the outside as I did before, but my inside spirit remains unchanged.

CHAPTER NINE

Another Christmas

In 1948 I was nineteen years old. The year was coming to a close with Christmas just around the corner. We all hoped we might have, at least on Christmas, a little joy and happiness, and some special food items that we otherwise would not have.

Life in East Germany under the Russian occupation was not easy. We were on food rations, and people had to stand in long lines in front of stores to get the daily things that give life—meat, fruit, vegetables, and other simple items. Often the store would run out of their supply, and the people must go home empty-handed and disappointed.

For special occasions, the government would supply the stores with bananas and oranges, which otherwise were not available for the people of East Germany. So it was that we were looking forward to the Christmas holiday and buying a few of these luxury items.

At this time, I discovered a red swelling on the top of my right foot. I showed it to my mother, and she thought I should see a doctor. So one evening I went with her to a clinic. The doctor looked at my foot and decided to operate immediately. He did not let me make an appointment for another day or another time, even though we were unprepared.

I soon found myself on an operating table. When I woke from the anesthesia, my foot was bandaged up. The next day, I was taken by ambulance to the city hospital. My foot was put in a cast with an opening on top of the foot, above the wound. I had a deep cut that was held open by some gauze so the pus could drain out. The wound was treated with penicillin. I was told that I had tuberculosis in my bone and my lungs. I was to be put in an isolation ward with other tuberculosis patients.

This was a disease that many people contracted after the war, because of our poor diets; a total lack of health-giving foods such as meat, milk, fruits, and vegetables. At the hospital, I was given food that was rich in protein and other good food that I had been deprived of for so many years.

Unfortunately I had no appetite and could not eat. This did not help my recovery. My foot did not improve. The flesh around the wound began to get black and necrotic. Every day when the nurses changed my dressings and cleaned the wound, my mother ran outside so she could not hear me scream.

I was also given calcium injections. Young nurses, who were still in training and were inexperienced, often missed my veins, causing my arm to be bruised, swollen, and sore.

One thing that happened that I cannot forget was a message of love and support from the members of our branch. One day the door opened, and standing in the corridor outside the room were members I knew. They began singing hymns of the Church. There were tears in my eyes to think they had brought this gift of music especially for me. No choir of angels could have sung more beautifully or been more appreciated.

Friends of my mother told her that I would not live until the next spring. This was a thought my mother could not bear. She went to the branch president and asked him to have the Elders give me a health blessing.

I received a blessing from the Elders. They promised me that I would survive and also keep my foot. Other patients, who shared the same room with me, had bone tuberculosis but lost their limbs by amputation because the wounds did not heal.

My mother at this time wrote a poem for me:

*My boy, when in times of trials and tribulations
    you asked, "Why me, Lord?"*
*Then listen to the still small voice of comfort that
    speaks to you,*
*Hold on with courage, and the Lord will not
    forsake you.*
As the sun breaks through the clouds of darkness,
And every night brings a new day of light,
So the Lord will do things right.
*Trust in Him, then no power of darkness can harm
    you.*
*In pain and suffering go to him, and pray with all
    your heart.*
He will never leave you alone.

As time went by, I lost my physical strength, but my spiritual strength was renewed. My faith and trust in the Lord never failed. I came closer to my Heavenly Father than at any other time in my life. I was dependent on His love to get me through the days. I relied on His arm of strength because I had none of my own.

I made a poster and put it on the wall next to my bed, with the words of Job: "The Lord has given it, the Lord has taken it away, blessed be the name of the Lord" (Job 1:21).

There was a day when I got out of bed against hospital orders. I was tired of using a bedpan and wanted to go to the toilet facility. I jumped down the hallway, slipped and fell, and hurt myself badly. I fell to one side and hit my head on the floor. Things went black, and for a few seconds I lost consciousness. I was in so much pain that I thought, lying there on the cold floor, it was the end for me. But finally I came to my senses enough to know that I was not going to die and I must go back to bed. There was no one around to help me. I crawled back to my room and somehow managed to get into the bed. There were no lasting effects from the fall, and I did not tell the nurses what I had done.

During my stay in the hospital, a nurse rolled a bed into our room. On it was a young man who was very ill with tuberculosis. We who shared the room were told that this young man was a prisoner who had been involved in robbery and also a murder. He was there for a checkup and was waiting his turn.

The other patients avoided this young man, but I went with my crutches to his bedside and began talking with him. After a while, he told me his story: how he had grown up on the streets and at an early age became part of a gang. All he had ever known was a life of crime under the influence of bad people. The things he told me were like a confession; the whole time, he cried, the tears running from his eyes onto the pillow.

I talked with him about my beliefs, about God, and His Son, Jesus Christ. It was the first time this young man had heard about God and Jesus Christ. While he was still weeping, his last words to me were: "If I had friends like you, I would not be in the situation where I am now."

He was moved out of our room a short time later. I have always been glad that I made the effort to befriend him. I had planted some seeds. Perhaps he would look for God and His Son, Jesus Christ, now that he knew of their existence.

There were eight patients in the isolated room. My mother brought my large poster paintings from home. I put them on the wall around the room so the men would have something to look at to cheer them. The pictures were of famous western movie stars.

Every morning when the doctors came in, they went first around the room and looked at the paintings. There were no pictures like that available in East Germany. The paintings were in black and white, except one I did in color of Maureen O'Hara. This was a favorite of my doctor. After admiring the paintings, the doctors then came to check their patients. When I was released from the hospital, I gave the Maureen O'Hara painting to my doctor. He was pleased to have it and thanked me profusely. When I began to get better I had my art supplies brought to me. I did a colored painting for each man in the room, which they were happy for.

The men in this room were older than I. They had endured much trouble in their lives, suffering through the Great Depression, the war, the troubled peace that turned out to be like the depression, except now we had the communist oppression to make our lives more miserable.

I was always a little bit crazy, born with a sense of humor that helped me get through the worst tragedies. I decided to try and cheer these men up a bit. I was like a clown in the circus. I had a large rubber cushion to sit on which prevented bedsores. It looked like a life preserver. When the nurse wheeled me from my small room into the ward where a bed was waiting for me, I put the cushion on my head and wore a clown face when I entered the room. Seeing me in this way, they all burst out laughing. It was probably the first laugh any of them had since entering the hospital.

I always tried to do things that would keep them cheered up. Once I made a painting of a man's head and put it on the pillow of an empty bed. We then rolled up blankets to look like a body and pulled the covers up. We called for the doctor to come quickly and look at this very sick man. The doctor came rushing in. When he saw what we had done, he laughed, and we then all had a good laugh.

I did drawings of all the men's faces. One night, two of

us went quietly into the women's ward and put these faces in the windows. When the women woke up in the morning, they thought men were staring at them through the windows. They were startled at first and began screaming; then they realized the joke and began laughing. The nurses laughed with them. We men were happy that a little joy came into sick people's lives that day.

I was released from the hospital almost a year after becoming a patient there. I walked on crutches for more than a year. For two years I walked with the help of a cane. I had scars on my lungs from the tuberculosis, and my right foot and leg were never normal again. Because no one helped with therapy in the hospital, my leg muscles atrophied, and the toes on my right foot became stiff and deformed. To this day, I have pain when walking. But I am grateful that I am otherwise healthy again and able to perform most physical activities as needed.

I put myself through a strenuous exercise program in order to regain my strength. When I was forty years old, I was tested in a sports program and received gold medals for several competitions: swimming, high jump, bicycle riding, and shot put.

As soon as I was able to get about on my own, I studied and passed the examination to be certified as a photo technician. I was employed. Because of my artistic ability, I also did retouching and photo restoration. Most of our customers were Russian. The men wanted us to do montages by taking their portrait photos, cutting off the heads, and mounting the head onto the body of someone who was wearing a suit, shirt, and tie. This was a sign of class for the poor Russians who had never owned a nice dark suit or a shirt and tie. We would then make a new negative and print the photo. I would also take separate photos of a man and a woman and mount them together so as to make them into a couple. The Russians paid with food items. Money had no value at that time because we could not buy anything with it.

The Russians always had food to eat, while we Germans starved. My boss had recently been in a POW camp. He had a heart for me and kindly shared the food the Russians brought.

CHAPTER TEN

One Last Fight for Freedom

I was twenty-three years old in 1952. I decided to leave my parents' home and the city of Cottbus. I wanted to move out in search of something better in life. I put an ad in the newspaper. A few weeks later I received several job offers. One was from a photo studio in the city of Leipzig. I chose this place because Leipzig had a well-known zoo. I loved animals and found joy and satisfaction from drawing animal pictures. Since I had never had the opportunity to sketch and draw those kinds of animals, this was where I wanted to go.

While living in Leipzig, I would often sit for hours on benches at the zoo drawing the big cats and the elephants. Years later, I became an accomplished wildlife artist, earning awards in contests and art shows.

In Leipzig, I worked for one year for a photo art company. I then went in together with another fellow, and we formed our own company. We mainly did hand coloring of black and white photos. This was a big business because thousands of Germans had lost loved ones in the war. A photograph was all they had left from their sons, fathers, or husbands. In the west, they had color photography by then, but we were quite far behind this new technology in the east.

Elsa followed me to Leipzig. We had been through so

much together and had developed a close relationship. Because of this, she wanted to be where I was. She soon found work and a room in an apartment house. We both enjoyed being in the big city of Leipzig. It is well-known for culture, art, and the annual trade show that attracted businesses from all over the world. Here Johann Sebastian Bach lived and worked and played the organ at the famed Thomas Church.

There was an LDS ward in the city also. We were happy attending our meetings there. One year later Elsa met a young man who was not a member of the church. She brought him to church, and he studied the gospel and became a member. Soon after this they married and had two children, first a boy and then a girl.

Life for the average German slowly began to improve. We seldom saw Russian soldiers on the street as we had in Cottbus. The Russians were quartered outside the town at many army bases. It was possible to almost forget the occupation and feel that we were breathing free air.

All this changed on June 17, 1953. This was a day none living in East Germany will ever forget. The government of East Germany began a new program of pushing people to work more hours, to work faster, and to produce more goods.

The Labor Department wanted the people to work on Saturday and Sunday with no days off. This campaign went on for a while, until the working class people decided not to take the abuse any longer. After years of hardship, suffering, and oppression, the people had enough. They did not go to work. They stood up against the Communist regime.

It began in Berlin. People left the factories and other places of work. They went outside and began marching in the streets. They carried banners demanding more free time, better conditions for the workers, more pay, and most of all, democracy with free elections.

When news about these demonstrations came out and

reached other cities, it began an avalanche of activity. One city after another followed the example of people in Berlin. The news was spread by radio, through a kind of underground communication network.

My partner was the first to bring the news on that morning. He was very excited, and so was I. My sister came to join with us in a protest march through the streets. In a big hurry, I wrote and printed hundreds of leaflets in our darkroom. Before they were completely dry, we took them out into the streets, where we handed them out among the crowds of people. Meanwhile, thousands of people in every city marched together, shouting, "Freedom! Solidarity!" My little fliers said, "Workers, show your solidarity with the people of Berlin! Go on strike!"

We handed the papers to anyone who would take them. On every street corner, more people joined with us. The protest grew larger and larger; like an army of giant ants, the people marched. Workers walked away from their jobs; among them were salespeople, scientists, doctors, nurses, engineers, students, housewives, and mothers holding the hands of their children. Some policemen showed up, but they were afraid to do anything against this mass of determined people.

It was the greatest, most euphoric feeling for all of us: after ten years of oppression, injustice, and suffering, to be able to stand and shout our feelings and raise our fists in anger against the hated Russian dictatorship.

In my life, I did not experience anything like this before or since—to see such joy and excitement among people who had so stoically borne oppression until that moment. The downtrodden population had been waiting for somebody with courage enough to spark the flame of freedom. Now this spark exploded; like an avalanche, nobody could stop its course.

We all felt that this was the hour of our freedom, the end of communism, and the downfall of a government no one had voted for and no one wanted. We expected the government to resign under this pressure from the people, and then we would once again have democracy.

What a joyous time it was at this great hour, when the people rose up and united, showing the world how we felt about the "government of the working class," and that the so-called "workers paradise" was in reality nothing more than a large prison.

Later in the day, people began singing songs of freedom and liberty. This was a tremendous demonstration of courage and love for our country. On the other side, the oppressors and their followers—the People's Police and the party members—must have feared that their time had come, and the regime of terror was over. They never showed their faces. They were hiding behind closed doors.

Students led the protesters to government buildings where large portraits of state and city government officials were on the walls. The students went inside and began tearing down the pictures of Marx, Engels, Stalin, and other party officials.

The crowd cheered in support and excitement, especially when the poster of the most hated man, Minister President Walter Ulbricht, came crashing down. People then began to tear and trample the posters under their feet.

We left the city center and began passing Grimmaische street when someone came forward with the old black, red, and gold flag of Germany, which we had before Hitler came into power. Instantly the crowd began to sing our former national anthem.

The army of protestors came to the largest hotel in Leipzig. Cooks in their white caps and uniforms came out and threw pictures of Communist leaders into the street. This was followed by shouts of joy and jubilation. No one was thinking about tomorrow.

Plaster busts of Communist leaders were smashed and party books burned. We did not know it, but plainclothes policemen were secretly filming some of the demonstrators. But with no hindrance from police or the military, we marched on, singing, shouting, and celebrating.

When we came to the Dimitroffplatz, the crowd stopped in front of a large stone building. This is where the political prisoners were kept. The multitude formed a large circle and began to yell, "Let the prisoners go free." First a few voices were heard, and then more and more voices were raised, until the sound of the crowd rose to a roar. "Let the prisoners go."

Nothing happened. Only a few frightened faces could be seen looking through barred windows. Some in the crowd picked up rocks and began throwing them. Glass windows shattered. Then there emerged from the building men wearing helmets and carrying rifles. Their faces were hard and showed no sign of mercy. They pointed their rifles at the human wall and began slowly walking closer with their guns leveled at the people who stood before them.

Where there had been deafening shouting only a moment before, now deadly silence hushed this huge mass of demonstrators. It was the calm before the storm. The unarmed people stepped back. Then the tension broke. Shots were fired. People were slammed to the ground. Some voices were heard crying, "Shame, shame . . . unarmed people . . . shame."

Another sound was then heard. The ground began to shake. People at the outer edge of the crowd started yelling, "Tanks! Tanks! Russian tanks! Run! Run!" Around the corner came the first huge Russian T34 with more following close behind. The sight of them spread unbelievable fear and terror. Like street sweepers, the tanks plowed directly into the fleeing masses of people—men, women, and children—without regard for any life.

A young woman next to me jumped over an iron fence

that was in front of a house. She became impaled by one of the sharp pointed spikes at the top of the fence. There was a deep cut in her thigh, and she began bleeding profusely.

At this same time, the Russians began to fire their big guns over the people's heads. What a frightful terrifying thing this was: the noise of the tanks rumbling behind us over the concrete street, the deafening explosions from the guns. We did not know as we ran if they were being aimed at us. We all ran for our lives, going in every direction to try to get away. This went on for some hours all over Leipzig. Everywhere there was chaos.

When the people were off the streets, driven behind walls, and the government was once more in control, a deadly silence descended like a dark cloud over the city.

* * *

At three o'clock in the afternoon, the government announced martial law over loud speakers. No more than three people were permitted to assemble in one place. No one could be on the streets after eight o'clock at night and not before six o'clock in the morning. This order was given with a warning that those who did not obey the law would be shot on the spot. Within twenty-four hours, the German Democratic Republic became once again a Russian zone.

The next morning, we heard that many citizens were arrested by the secret police. They had gone from house to house during the night and taken people away.

The people of East Germany could not understand why the government of the United States stood by during this time and did nothing to help us in our struggle for freedom. We needed help in our uprising against the oppressors, but no one in the world outside came to our aid. We felt alone and totally forsaken. This was when we began as a people to lose all hope that things could get better. The United States Army was just across the border, but they did not interfere as the Russians began killing and imprisoning more and more of the German people. We had gained nothing except to bring our plight to the attention of the world. Our sweet dream of freedom burst like a soap bubble.

Minister President Walter Ulbricht declared to the world, "The uprising was the work of some agents and saboteurs from the West. They threw the torch, and it fell on flammable grounds."

During the next days and weeks, many more people were arrested. The Russian government realized that they must put out even the smallest spark of freedom that burned in the hearts of the people.

The dreaded KGB had ways of recruiting and winning the cooperation of thousands of ordinary citizens. The secret police in East Germany used threats and blackmail to force people to work for them. They found their spies among housewives, teachers, workers, and students in school who were brainwashed at early ages to spy on their families. They were like a penetrating fog creeping into the life of the German people.

One such example involved a young girl who was a member of our church. Her father was arrested after the war and put into one of the most feared prisons, a former fortress in the city of Bautzen. He now was kept in this place for political prisoners because he had once been a member of the official Nazi party. These prisoners were treated very badly, much worse than other prisoners. The man was not a member of the Church, but his wife and two daughters were.

One day, the secret police came to the apartment of this man's family when the youngest daughter, Evelyn, was home alone. They wanted her to spy on members of the LDS branch in Cottbus. They tried to pressure her to work for them. If she would do it, they promised to let her father go home and be a free man. But Evelyn refused to betray the members of the Lord's church.

The officers kept at her and tried to force her to sign a paper saying she would become a government spy. Finally, she could no longer resist. With tears running from her eyes, she took the pen and tried to sign her name. But the pen did not work. It would not make a mark. This was for Evelyn a sign from God not to sign the paper. She then absolutely refused, and the officers realized it was useless to try further. They left without her signature on the paper.

Evelyn kept a clear conscience and received a burning testimony that the Lord lived and was mindful of her. He had shown her in a miraculous way what is right.

There were spies everywhere. You could not trust even your best friend. Children betrayed their own parents, thinking they did what was best for their country. The police wanted information about every aspect of the citizen's lives: where they went, what they read, what they listened to on the radio, who their friends were, and what they talked about in the privacy of their homes.

Almost anything one did could be turned into a crime that he or she would be punished for. One of these crimes was listening to the western radio station RIAS—Radio im Amerikanischen Sector—which could be heard all over Europe. Secretly, we all listened to this station, but if the police knew, we would be arrested.

It was also forbidden to read anything not approved by the Communist government.

The same was true of movies, plays, or theatre productions. You also could not write, print, or paint anything that was not permitted by the state. Everything was controlled by the government except our own thoughts—and the air waves.

When television came to East Germany, anyone who

owned a set watched the news and other programs coming from the West. The Communist government tried very hard to interrupt these short waves by building towers that would send out signals designed to scramble the short waves. But the people found ways to avoid this interference—they would install extra antennas and direct them toward the west.

The police would go from house to house, looking for antennas pointed toward the west. The people living there would then be arrested. Eventually the police gave up on this; they could not arrest all the people who committed this "crime."

The uprising worsened the condition of East German people by a large degree. Martial law was strictly enforced. There was no right of assembly. Other new restrictions and rules became law.

The government of West Germany declared June 17 a national day to remember the uprising of the East German people. It was designated as a day of mourning for all those who had died or were imprisoned because of their yearnings for liberty and democracy, those who wanted the right to choose their own type of government through free elections.

What the Communists called "elections" were nothing more than an undemocratic way for the ruling class to stay in power without the consent of the people.

In reality, citizens were forced to go to the polling places and put slips in the boxes. There were no secret ballots and no choice; the only candidates were members of the Communist party nominated by their own government. Party members would go from place to place looking for those who had not voted. They were then forced to do their duty as a citizen. The final result was that the Communist party received 99 percent of the people's votes.

The government, the party, and the candidates could then celebrate victory and declare to the world that the people of East Germany were behind them. After living fifteen years under Nazi dictatorship and another fifteen years under the Communist regime, East Germans realized there was absolutely no difference.

The Communists and Nazis used the same methods to obtain their goals. Both governments tried everything to win the young people over through indoctrination that began in kindergarten and continued on through high school and college. However, the Communists used a much more intense form of brainwashing. Young people listened to the same propaganda day after day all their lives.

Both governments had the same kind of youth organizations; boys and girls had to be members. They had no choice of what to read, see, or hear. In school, atheism and Marxism were taught. Freedom of religion was guaranteed by the so-called "Constitution." In reality, there was no freedom of anything. If the school faculty discovered that a student still believed in God and went to church, that person would be ridiculed in front of the student body. No one who went to church and believed in God would be admitted to high school or college if it were known. This person also could not find a good job at companies owned by the state.

An occurrence at an elementary school was told in our church. A teacher at a young boy's school preached the government explanation about evolution as was required by the state school board. The teacher then asked if anyone still believed in God. Only one student raised his hand: an LDS boy.

The teacher told this student that his homework was to write down fifty times, "There is no God." The boy came home and told his mother. She told her son not to do the assignment. The next day, the teacher told the boy that now he must write this sentence one hundred times before he could come back to school. When the boy went home, his mother was incensed. The next morning, she went to school with her son.

She went to the principal and demanded to see the teacher who had assigned such a thing to her boy. The principal told her she could not see the teacher because he had died the night before.

The God that the Communists believed in, worshipped, and prayed to was Joseph Stalin. Children in kindergarten were taught songs praising him. They were also taught to declare their devotion and admiration for him. What Adolf Hitler had been to the Nazis, Joseph Stalin was to the Communists.

The day Stalin died, my sister and I were browsing through a large, state-owned department store in Leipzig. Over the intercom came the news that the "Great Leader of the Soviet Union" had just passed away. The store manager asked the shoppers for a minute of silence to show their respect. People obediently stopped and stood silent. No one moved or spoke a word. This was too much for my sister and me. We kept on with our business as if we had not heard.

This is the way the two of us were. I often said things that, if reported, could land me in prison. My mother lived in constant fear for my safety because of this.

CHAPTER ELEVEN

Serving a Mission

My family and I did not believe in any aspect of the Communist government, but we followed the admonition of the Church that is stated in the Twelfth Article of Faith: "We believe in being subject to kings, presidents, rulers, and magistrates, in obeying, honoring, and sustaining the law."

The East German government looked favorably upon members of our faith, because, despite the terrible conditions under which we lived, we were good, honest citizens and reliable workers who did not smoke or drink. For these reasons, we were allowed to hold our meetings and some other activities. But every meeting must be planned and reported in advance to the police. They must know who the speakers were and what their subject matter would be.

Missionary work was permitted only by our own people and within our country. I was called to serve a mission from 1956 to 1958. I was twenty-seven years old at the start.

Sometimes when we were in a town, we missionaries would be taken to a police station and told that we were forbidden to proselyte. But my companion and I were not easily intimidated. I would remind the officers that our state constitution guaranteed us freedom to practice our religion. I then asked for a written statement forbidding us to do our job as missionaries, but, of course, they dared not do that.

We knew that the local governments watched us closely, hoping to find some reason for shutting the Church down. We therefore must be doubly careful of what we said and did. Baptismal services were performed in public places—a lake or a river.

While serving in Thuringia, we needed to baptize a young man, his mother, and an elderly woman. It was November, and in this part of the country, it was extremely cold. The river we had to use was formed by streams coming from the high mountains of the Brocken. On Saturday morning, I went into the river to test the place and find the right spot.

The freezing water stunned me. I rushed back to the river bank. I wondered how we were going to withstand the frigid water long enough to baptize three people and how the elderly woman, who had asthma and heart problems, would survive being put under the water. If anything untoward happened that would be the end of our little branch in Thuringia.

On Sunday, we went ahead with the baptismal service. We trusted in the Lord and prayed for His blessing. All went as planned. The elderly woman was not harmed by the cold river water; when she came out, she said, "I did not feel a thing." This was another testimony to me of God watching over, and protecting faithful believers wherever they are in the world. People who were not members gathered to watch what we did. We could tell that they thought we were all insane.

There were times when we had to chop holes in frozen lakes for baptisms. We carried one woman who was very sick into freezing water, and she walked out by herself.

During my mission, all the missionaries came together for a conference at the city of Eisenach. This is the famous old city in Germany where Martin Luther was "captured" and retained for his safety in the Wartburg fortress (castle) belonging to his friend and benefactor, King Friedrich der

Weise. While living there, Martin Luther translated most of the Bible into German, and in this building he wrote the ninety-five propositions that he tacked to the big doors of the Schlosskirche at Wittenberg.

Monks still reside in the old fortress, which is reached by riding a donkey. During our conference, we missionaries also one day rode donkeys up the mountain to visit the famous ancient building.

In the city of Bernburg, I met an elderly woman who told me that her husband had been in the concentration camp at Schwiebus. He was allowed to go home because of sickness. He told her that of the two thousand prisoners shipped to Siberia by train, only eighty survived. Had I not escaped, I would have been one of the two thousand. I never knew what happened to those young people from Landsberg who were imprisoned with me.

I served nearly three years as a missionary and was honorably released. I was the last person called to serve a Church mission in East Germany. No new missionaries were allowed to be called after that.

CHAPTER TWELVE

Circus Life

I was now at a crossroads in my life. I was thirty years old, without responsibilities or commitments. I decided to fulfill one of my boyhood dreams. I wanted to become a lion tamer in the circus.

I grew up with knowledge of circus life because there was a circus that had its winter quarters in Landsberg. They traveled by railroad. Each year, when I knew of their arrival, I ran to watch the animals being unloaded: the lions, tigers, horses, and zebras. Especially I loved to see the elephants and hear their loud trumpeting. The sights and sounds were wonderful to me.

I breathed it all into my system, loving every minute of everything that happened. I hung around there every day that I could. Sometimes trainers would let me clean the stalls, bring water, and whatever else needed doing. By this, I earned tickets to get inside the big tent where people were performing, training, and practicing new acts for the next year. When I had no ticket, I would crawl under the tent and watch until the coast was clear and then go sit on the bleachers. I never got enough of it. It seemed such a romantic world.

I applied for a job as an animal keeper at the famous Circus Busch. This was a world-renowned circus for many years. After the war, the Communist government confiscated it from the owners. I got the job and left for East Berlin where the circus's winter quarters were located.

To become a trainer, you start from the bottom as assistant to the trainer in taking care of the animals. You feed the animals, keep their stalls and cages clean, and in this way get to know the animals. You watch the trainer and how he works, and someday when the trainer is unable to perform during the show due to an accident or injury, you get your chance to replace the trainer. This was what I was hoping would happen to me.

It was not long before I realized that circus life was not as rosy as I had thought. When I arrived, I was assigned to care for the horses. There was a beautiful white horse named Morus that I liked. Whenever I got close to Morus, he would reach out and grab my shirt with his lips, pulling me close to him. In a short time, I was reassigned as elephant keeper. I loved the elephants—the big gentle giants of God's creation. I cared for two elephants, and another young man cared for the other two. While working with the elephants, we also had to assist our boss during the circus performances. We were dressed in nice uniforms of black pants and a red vest.

I formed a close relationship with my two charges, especially the one named Gitta. I spent my free time with her while my co-workers were drinking and partying. I won the trust of the animals because I treated them with love and respect. I never punished them without a reason.

Before we took the elephants out to the ring, they had to be cleaned. Sometimes, after she was clean, Gitta would throw straw or hay on her back. I then commanded her to sit down for a few minutes. She did not like this punishment. When I let her up again, she would grip me around the neck with her trunk and pull me close. She could have choked and killed me in a second. But I was not afraid of her. She would always let me go after she had shown her power.

Our boss, Epi Vidane, the trainer who performed with them, was a short little man from Ceylon. He had grown up with elephants. He had very dark skin and a mouthful of shiny gold teeth. He smiled a lot to show them off. During his performances, he would remove his white turban and put his head in the mouth of Jenny, another of the elephants. Jenny would march around the ring with her trainer's head in her mouth. I wanted to prove to myself that I could do the same thing with Gitta. One day when we were alone, I did put my head in her mouth. I had complete trust in her that she would not hurt me. My trust was rewarded; she did not close her mouth while my head was in it.

In the spring, we and our four elephants were shipped to the Czech Republic, where we joined up with a circus. From the railroad stations, we marched through the narrow streets of small towns to show off the animals and let people know the circus was there. The children were very excited. They would come running, shouting, "Slonies! Slonies!" (meaning elephants).

One day while I was sitting on top of Gitta brushing and cleaning her, I dropped the brush I was using. I sat there thinking, *Now, I have to go down and get it and climb back up again.* But as I was thinking this, Gitta picked up the brush and handed it back to me.

There were often times when it was dangerous to work with elephants. They were easily spooked by almost anything. They then became wild and uncontrollable. Sometimes this happened in the middle of the night. After being awakened by their trumpeting and screaming, I would rush out and try to calm them down. Usually it was a dog or cat that had frightened them. When elephants are excited, they let go of their bladders; it sounds like a waterfall, and the air is filled with a steaming odor.

The elephant named Jenny that our boss worked with in the ring hated Gitta and tried to kill her one day when I was bringing her back from watering. Jenny got away from me and rammed her large head into the side of Gitta, who was much smaller. At the same moment, I was pushed between the two animals and in danger of being crushed to death. The trainer and others rushed to help me.

At the same stable we had a Hungarian steer named Mohatsch. He was at the circus only for show. He was the wildest and most dangerous animal I ever saw, but he was also the most beautiful one. He had very long horns, curly dark brown hair between the ears, and big black eyes that shone like diamonds, with long silky lashes. None of the workers liked having him as part of the circus because he was such a menace.

Mohatsch was fastened to the wall in his stall by a rope tied to the ring in his nose. No one could go near him. His reflexes were lightning fast; you could be snared by one of his long horns or kicked by his powerful legs. When we moved on to the next city, it took twelve men to transport him from his stall to the train car, six men on each side holding the ropes that were in his nose ring.

I fell in love with the steer and wanted to win his trust. When I was alone, I would softly talk to him and just let him look at me. One day a worker came too close to the animal and was gored. Then even more of the circus workers began to hate and fear Mohatsch. They wanted to kill the beast, but they could not do it without permission from the state government.

I came one day into his stall and realized with horror that the rope was loose and had come out of the wall. If the steer realized he was free, he would run through the stables causing havoc wherever he went, scaring the other animals and goring them with his horns. The elephants would then stampede, creating pandemonium and destruction. At that moment, I knew I had to get the rope refastened before Mohatsch realized he was not attached to the wall.

I said a silent fervent prayer; then moving slowly, I went to the front of the animal and fastened the rope just inches away from the long pointed horns; I was sweating and praying the whole time. To this day, I believe that another miracle happened when I was able to come that close to Mohatsch without being gored or trampled to death.

Another animal we had in a cage just for show was a wolf. He was ferocious and mean in a different way from Mohatsch. No one dared go near his cage. He would show his yellow teeth, hiss, and growl. His eyes were filled with hate, and he looked like he wanted to tear anyone apart who came close. I thought that he had been treated badly by some animal handlers, causing him to be consumed with hatred for people.

It became a challenge for me to try to gain the trust of this poor creature that must have gone through some terrible experiences. Maybe I could understand because of what I had suffered in my life. I began going to his cage and just talking quietly to him. After a while, he did not growl at me or bare his teeth. Then I had the courage to put my hand through the bars of the cage. He rolled over on his back, and I rubbed his belly like a puppy dog. We were friends.

Circus people are different—a special kind of human being. They are like a big family, each caring for the other one. Everybody is thought of as equal and treated that way. In cases of emergency, such as when we were surprised by a sudden storm, which would often happen in the night, everybody helped out. You could see the trapeze artist or the high-wire performer working side by side with truck drivers and animal keepers to secure and tighten the ropes that were holding the big tent in place.

On pleasant occasions such as weddings or birthdays,

all the circus performers attended the celebration. The circus band provided the music; the clowns, the entertainment. Elephants would carry the bride or birthday person, and with their trunks they presented the flowers. This was all a special show just for the circus family.

One of my own sweetest memories during this time happened on a Sunday morning. While the other people were sleeping, I went into the big tent and played and sang our most beloved Church hymns at the piano. At that time, I felt very close to the Lord and His spirit of comfort and love.

Another special memory is when our train traveled through the countryside; I sat outside on the rear platform and played my harmonica. Feelings of peace and beauty nearly overwhelmed me during those times.

Our tour ended at the famous old city of Prague. Again we went with our elephants from the train station to the city center. We were greeted there by the mayor and other important citizens, as well as people from the news media.

From the big hotel nearby came an elegantly dressed waiter carrying a silver tray. On the tray were glasses of champagne for us. While the cameras were rolling, my boss, the elephant trainer, stepped up to the waiter and pointed at me. With his loud voice, in broken German, he shouted, "Oh, no. He not drink alkohl!" Then he was laughing and showing his gold teeth. The waiter went back and brought me a glass of orange juice. The little man from Ceylon knew about my religion and respected it.

Wherever I was, I kept the Word of Wisdom. I was never ashamed of being different in that way. When I worked for a company in Heidelberg, there was a big party. While the boss was talking to all the employees, they raised their bottles of beer for a toast. The manager came and handed me a baby bottle filled with milk. The assembled workers roared with laughter, and so did I. Then I drank the milk. A short time later when there was an election for work counsel chairman, I received 90 percent of the votes.

While I was stationed at Prague with the circus, a brother from our Church came to see me. He had been given my address by the mission president, Henry Burkhardt. At this time, the government of Czechoslovakia did not allow members of the LDS Church to assemble. They met in secret at someone's apartment. We went there together for Sunday services. A group of six sisters were there. They had not seen an elder of the Church for a long time and had been unable to partake of the sacrament. They asked me to bless and pass the sacrament to them.

I did not have my scriptures with me and had no text for the sacrament prayer, but I could not disappoint the Savior's faithful little flock. As so often I had done through the years of terror and bondage, I relied upon the Lord. I knelt and bowed my head and prayed for the words to come. I then blessed the bread and water and passed it to the grateful sisters. Afterward a sister presented her little child to me and asked that she be blessed, which I did.

On Christmas Eve, I volunteered to watch the animals while the other circus workers had a party downtown. I was alone in the stable with the horses, camels, zebras, and elephants. Sitting on a bale of hay, I played my beloved Christmas hymns on the harmonica. As I played, I thought of the Savior and His humble birth among the beasts in a stable.

Then came the brother whom I had met before. He brought me a bag full of homemade cookies. We wished each other a peaceful Christmas and spent a few quiet moments of brotherhood together.

I had gathered treats of apples and carrots for my four-legged friends. After I had fed them, I sat on my bale of straw, and we continued to enjoy our private celebration. I ate my cookies, and the animals munched their fruit and vegetables.

* * *

Circus work was very hard, especially for me. I had not been used to such heavy, manual labor. My co-workers and I had to set up the tents for our elephants. We used twelve-pound hammers to drive iron anchors into the hard ground. These anchors held the ropes of the tent. We were three young men who worked in unison to pound the anchors into the ground. It had to be done in an exact rhythm, one blow following another. If any one of us missed the anchor, his leg would be smashed to pieces.

When we left a place, we removed the anchors, took down the tent, and loaded everything on a truck. To lift and load the tent was the heaviest hardest work I had ever done, but I kept up with the other men, who were younger and stronger than I. Once again I believe that the Lord gave me the strength to do my job and protected me from harm.

In my free time, I volunteered to help the woman trainer of lions. I did this in order to find a way of reaching my goal to become an animal trainer. I also assisted the trainer of tigers. But my hopes for climbing the circus success ladder were dashed when, one morning as I was climbing out of the tigers's cage, the heavy iron door slid down from above and hit my right middle finger, cutting off the top of it. I had to go home for surgery, and the circus left on tour without me.

At this time, I also had the feeling that the Lord did not want me to go back to the circus because I could not keep the Sabbath day holy as I should.

CHAPTER THIRTEEN

Freedom

In the spring of 1961, I went home again to the city of Cottbus. Life in East Germany was still the same. Joseph Stalin had been replaced by another dictator, a man named Kruschev, who ruled with an iron fist over all East European nations. Like before, the people of East Germany had no control over their own destiny.

Now even greater numbers of desperate people were trying to escape to the west. Some were killed in the effort. So great was the desire for freedom that people were willing to risk their lives. Every year it became more and more difficult to escape. From east to west, the borders were protected by mine fields, attack dogs, barbed wire, and heavily armed guards. The last place left for escape was Berlin.

Traffic between East and West Berlin was still open, and according to the agreement between Allied Forces, it was to be kept open. People who went from East Berlin to the other side were searched—all belongings, bags, and suitcases. If the guards found anything of a suspicious nature, that person would be arrested; if there was proof that an escape had been attempted, they went to prison for many years.

Before the subways left the east moving to the western sector, the guards would step out, and the subways were taken over by guards and personnel from the west.

In May 1961, I had the feeling that I must leave East Germany before it was too late. I could not tell anybody about my decision because I did not want to endanger my family or friends. According to the law, anyone who knew someone who wanted to escape was obligated to report this person to the police; otherwise, he or she would be arrested for conspiracy.

I bought a new camera outfit—one of the best with an extra telephoto and wide-angle lens. I intended to sell it in the west to have some money. I also packed my typewriter that was of great value to me. These items in my suitcase would, when discovered, definitely put me in suspicion of trying to escape. But I trusted in my good fortune and prayed mightily that I might one more time be blessed to carry out my plans.

I took the train from Cottbus to Berlin. A guard insisted on opening my suitcase. He passed over everything except my Book of Mormon, which was sitting on top in plain sight. He picked it up as if he had really found something. The book was over a hundred years old and not on the forbidden list for Germans. But the guard was new and did not know what to make of this book. He looked through the pages and, finally, decided to confiscate it. I smiled inside, hoping he would read it and discover what a treasure he had. He indicated that I could close my suitcase and moved away with the book.

Just before arriving in Berlin, the guards came in and checked our passports. You could not go anywhere in East Germany without carrying identification. I was confident because the last address in the passport showed Berlin-Hoppegarten and Circus Busch. Circus people still had some freedom left, and I counted on this to get me through.

When the guards had looked through my passport they handed it back and did not search my suitcase. After a while, which seemed like an eternity, the train moved on. The people in my compartment began to breathe with relief. Tension was broken, the fear gone.

This was my fourth and last escape from the Communists. I was finally free. The Iron Curtain that had kept me imprisoned for fifteen years was behind me. I had dreamed of this day for such a long time, always wondering if I could make it happen, and here I was: I had passed every check point and was riding on the train toward freedom. This was my fourth and last escape.

At the border in West Berlin, I was interviewed by American intelligence officers, as all escapees from East Germany were. I then went to a refugee camp. After my case was processed, I received official papers and was permitted to stay in the Federal Republic of Germany.

I went to the famous and beautiful city of Heidelberg. I had a friend living there. We were former missionary companions. He had escaped several years earlier while I was traveling with the circus. In Heidelberg, I found an LDS ward, made good friends, and got a job with the United States Corps of Engineers. My work was making maps for the United States Army in Europe and for NATO. I was there eight years until the time came that German workers had to be laid off.

A short time later, I was accepted by the University of Heidelberg as a scientific illustrator. The university is over five hundred years old and very famous in the world. At the same time I attended the Art Academy at Karlsruhe. After two years I graduated with the highest degree. My work was published in books, and my large posters were used as teaching aids by the Heidelberg University.

In 1963, to celebrate becoming a worldwide church, the LDS Church announced a contest for members of the church from all parts of the world to write stories from their personal experience having to do with religion. I heard about this contest at the end of a general conference broadcast and decided

111

to send the story that I had written about the young prisoner who I met at the hospital.

I won second place and received a complimentary letter from one of the Church leaders. One day, most unexpectedly, there came to me from America a large package. I was filled with wonder at this. Inside a box was the prize I had not known I earned from the contest: twelve recordings of the Tabernacle Choir. I could not believe my eyes—such an unbelievable treasure this was. I cannot forget the wonder of hearing for myself, whenever I wanted to, music from this glorious choir. Certainly, no other person living in Germany had such a precious gift.

While I lived in this beautiful, romantic city of Heidelberg, I had a wonderful experience with one of God's beautiful creatures. I lived close enough to walk to church. It was wintertime. The streets and sidewalks were covered with black ice. One Sunday morning, when I was walking along the Neckar River on my way to church, I had just crossed the bridge when I saw a large, white swan in the middle of the street. I realized that the big bird was in trouble. Evidently it had flown out of the river, landed on the slippery ice, and could not get to its feet, which prevented it from flying away. The bird was also in danger of being hit by an automobile.

Swans are known to be very aggressive toward humans. Their wings are so strong they can easily break a person's arms or legs. Knowing this, I still decided to try and help the swan. I slowly approached and picked him up in my arms. He was very heavy, probably weighing forty pounds. I carried the bird down to the river. When he saw the water, he jumped from my arms and flew to the middle of the river, where he landed and was happily greeted by his family. I had a good, happy feeling knowing that I was able to save this beautiful creature from harm.

A few years later, while still employed at the university, I fulfilled another of my childhood dreams and became a glider pilot. The training school for glider pilots was situated in the Rhoen mountain range, surrounded by hills and forests. It was located on top of a mountain called the Wasserkuppe. It was the oldest and most famous school in Germany for training glider pilots, near the city of Fulda, close to the East German border. The flight instructor warned us to stay away from East German air space.

When I was soaring in a glider like an eagle in the wind, looking down from above, I had the first idea of how God must feel. I was free from all the shackles that bind humans on earth. This was real freedom, without guards, fences, mine fields, or Russian tanks. I always hated to end a flight and come back to earth.

There was one drop of bitterness in my cup of happiness. I could not forget my loved ones and the friends I had left behind, who still had to suffer through life behind the Iron Curtain. Even sometime later in my life, I would feel guilty for having run away, instead of staying to share oppression with the people in East Germany. My mother, however, was happy for me and also relieved because now she did not have to worry about my safety.

In August 1961, things in East Germany began to change drastically for the people.

In open violation of the Potsdam Agreement between the four occupying armed forces; the Russians, one early morning, began the first steps to cut East Berlin away from West Berlin. First they rolled barbed wire across the streets. When the citizens of Berlin got up and wanted to go to work, they were trapped and could not go anywhere.

It was unbelievable to everyone. The whole western world was shocked to realize that the Russians would do something so brutal and egregious without concern for the well-being of the people.

Families were now separated, friends and loved ones kept apart, and streets divided.

The people cried and pleaded with the guards to let them go home or to work; they argued and demanded, but to no avail. The guards followed the instructions they had been given by the Communist government.

The United States Army was there, only yards away; they stood ready to defend Berlin and the rights of its people; they waited for word from their top leadership. But no word of protest came from that government—no action, no help for the people of East Berlin. America did not want to tangle with the mighty Russian Bear and was afraid of offending. The East Germans looked up to the United States government as their protector, but just as before, during the people's uprising in 1953, the Americans did nothing, and once again the helpless people felt betrayed.

A short time later, Russian tanks and armored vehicles came on the scene. With this blatant show of military force, the people knew that their last bastion of freedom was closing. They made desperate attempts at escaping. They ran and jumped across the razor-sharp barbwire, helped by people on the other side. Some made it to freedom; others were caught in the wires. Some were shot and killed on the spot by border guards. Some guards threw away their rifles and jumped over the fences themselves.

Among the many young people who tried to escape during those first days was one young man named Peter Fechter. His sad story was shown on television all over the free world. He ran and jumped over the fence. While he was still in the no man's land between two borders, he was shot by the guards and wounded. He lay there slowly bleeding to death. No one came to his rescue for fear that they too would be shot. He pleaded with people from the west to come and save him, but nobody did. They watched his agony and did nothing. After he was dead, the East German guards pulled his lifeless body through the sand and away from sight.

Ever after that, the name Peter Fechter became a symbol known among all people who are oppressed and struggle for freedom. Near the site of his death, a small bronze plaque was erected, to remind the world of these tragic events that took place two months after my escape from East Germany.

The Communist Peoples Army then began to build with concrete the shameful Berlin Wall, which became a symbol of oppression, inhumanity, and all else that is evil about a system that needed to use walls, tanks, and guns against unarmed citizens in order to stay in power. The government stated that the wall was necessary to keep out agents, terrorists, and other criminal elements from the West.

Even with the wall up some people tried to escape; a few made it. Others, who were not so lucky, were arrested or killed. Families who were separated from loved ones would bring ladders to the wall and look over to where, on the other side, their friends and relatives, with tears running down their cheeks, waved white towels. This was one of the saddest chapters in the history of the so-called German Democratic Republic.

Later, when President Reagan visited West Berlin, he came to the wall and looked over to the east. He told the world that if anyone would like to see what communism is like, let him come to Berlin and look at this wall. He then added harsh words to the Soviet leader, telling him, "Mr. Gorbachev, tear down this wall!"

* * *

Ten years later after my escape, I met Linda Trinny, a beautiful young woman from California who was serving a mission in Southern Germany for the LDS Church. I was with an LDS entertainment group going to different wards to perform. When we were at the ward in the town of Karlsruhe, Linda was there. She and her companion were serving in that area.

We talked together after the program and found that we had many interests in common. We had similar tastes in music—we both enjoyed the old folk songs and classical music. She was a singer too, with a sweet voice. The biggest surprise was that she had a pilot's license and loved to fly. This seemed too good to be true. I had waited all this time to find the girl of my dreams. It was love almost immediately for both of us. We exchanged addresses and corresponded.

I was forty-one years old and did not want to wait any longer to be married. Linda received special permission from her mission president to be released from her mission. He was happy for us and encouraged the marriage. She received her temple recommend at that time also. We were married at the city hall of Schwetzingen and drove that day to Switzerland, where we were married in the Swiss Temple. I then returned with her to the United States of America.

In October 1971, we arrived on the *SS France* late at night in the New York harbor. The next morning, when everyone was still asleep I went alone on deck and was greeted by a famous old lady. She was stretching her arm toward the sky with her shining torch—the Statue of Liberty. What a sight for me to see that marvelous, giant piece of art standing high above—a symbol of liberty, justice, and happiness for all people of the world.

This was my last and final step on a long and often dangerous road to freedom. I silently thanked God for His wise counsel and watchful eye throughout the journey.

Epilogue

Five years later, I was sworn in as an American citizen and proudly pledged allegiance to the flag and to the Republic. I was then free to return to East Germany and visit the family and friends I had left behind. I was no longer afraid to cross the border into East Germany because I was under the protection of the United States.

Ten years later, in 1989, the world witnessed one of the greatest miracles in our lifetime. The wall of shame and Soviet oppression, the hated Berlin Wall, came crumbling down, piece by piece. After twenty-eight years, standing as a reminder of the terrible injustice of the Communist regime that took place in 1961, the monument of terror fell apart, just as did the government that had erected it.

Two great leaders, Ronald Reagan and Mikhail Gorbachev, were responsible for the little stone to begin rolling into an avalanche that no one could stop. Strong winds of change blew away old ways of thinking. Across the wall, East met West and came together after forty-three years of separation. The divided nation became again one Germany. We who lived in the East never thought that would happen in our lifetime.

The most incredible fact was that the strong, mighty wall came down without one shot being fired, without one drop of blood being shed. Young people from the West climbed on top of the wall and raised their hands in the sign of victory. They helped those on the other side by pulling them up while others pushed from below.

Others were seen using sledgehammers and pickaxes to try to break down the wall, but the reinforced concrete was too strong, and only small pieces came off. While this was going on, the guards from both sides watched the excited masses and did not know what to do or how to react.

The next days were filled with celebration: of dancing in the streets, of drinking, of laughing, and of crying. This was a time of great joy and happiness. For the first time in twenty-eight years, Berliners could walk from East to West and from West to East. Friends, loved ones, and relatives could visit each other again.

Later the wall was demolished by heavy equipment and hauled away in trucks.

The week-long celebration ended with a combined symphony orchestra from East and West Germany, with a choir of many hundreds of voices. All were seated under the famous old Brandenburg Gate, which had survived the bombing and shelling during World War II, when the entire city of Berlin was destroyed.

The concert ended with the orchestra playing Ludwig ven Beethoven's Ninth Symphony and the choir singing. No words could better express the feelings of the people on that night than the great freedom-loving German poet Friedrich von Schiller, who wrote the words to the Ninth Symphony:

Sing to joy and gladness now and ever more to freedom's song. Open up your hearts desire with love that's everlasting. Let this magic bring together all who dwell upon the earth. All mankind shall be together and peace shall reign upon the earth. May the joy of brotherhood spread throughout the Universe. Then the very air we breathe shall be pure, calm and gentle. Blue the sky and green the forest, all our children can run free. And through music bring together all who sing the ode to joy.

The famous conductor Leonard Bernstein changed the word "joy" to "freedom." Thus the "ode to joy" became the "ode to freedom."

The human spirit triumphed at last over the forces of evil. The Soviet Union disintegrated and communism ended; this began in Russia and spread to all the other East European nations that had been ruled by Russia.

My explanation for these momentous events that took place so unexpectedly is simple: "God moves in a mysterious way His wonders to perform; He plants his footsteps in the sea and rides upon the storm."

Werner Klein's Art Biography

Scientific illustrator for the University of Heidelberg.

Artist in Residence at the University of Heidelberg.

Scientific illustrations published in universities throughout Germany.

Member of the Napa Valley Art Association.

Napa Valley Art Association—won Best Picture five times.

Davis County Art Exhibit—won a ribbon for Best Theme.

Davis County Art Exhibit—won the People's Choice award.

In 2004, for the second time, his work was chosen from many entries to go on a traveling show throughout the Utah.

Won many awards for wildlife paintings at different art exhibits.